Outboards:
80 Years of Reminiscence
Volume 1

Written by Lawrence C. Carpenter

Edited by
Lincoln Davis and
Ann-Marie Carpenter

It has been a long time since I carried outboard motors up the steep back stairway to the attic, or rather the loft, of our old New Hampshire farmhouse built about the time George Washington passed away. Once there, the motor would be placed against a pale blue backdrop, the lighting positioned, wife Ann-Marie would take the photo and then develop the film in her adjoining darkroom. She would also type my handwritten text and the column would go out to Trailer Boats Magazine hopefully prior to that month's deadline.

After writing a couple feature articles for the magazine it was kind of decided by Editor Jim Youngs, Publisher Ralph Poole and myself that I would write a monthly column on antique outboard motors, or occasionally other marine subject matter. The first column appeared in the 1981 May issue and through many changes at TBM was carried until the end of 1994.

In the years since I had thought of gathering everything together under a single cover, but that never happened. This volume is totally the product of AOMCI member Lincoln Davis and family. All I did was supply the original typed unedited manuscripts, most of the photos and sketches plus a set of the related magazines for any needed reference. Like most projects, it was a lot more work than anticipated and I thank him for carrying it through to its very productive end.

Larry Carpenter

Editor's Note:

My life has been one long pursuit to resolve outboard motorboat challenges. That's why I've always searched for the honest evaluation of all marine products: boats, outboards, inboards and everything in between. In the late 1980's, that pursuit led me to Trailer Boat Magazine. That magazine had real mechanics evaluating the engines. And if there was a risk in offending an advertiser with a review, well, I liked how you could read between the lines. The very best part of the magazine for me was "The Antique Corner" by Larry Carpenter. I studied Carpenter's articles because knew I could trust his knowledge to work for me on my antique projects.

I can't exactly remember how our friendship began, but maybe it was a meet he had at his place, but over the years of outboard events, we became friends. When Larry's articles stopped at the end of 1994, I lost a lot of enthusiasm for the magazine. I stopped subscribing altogether when Trailer Boat Magazine was sold to a marine publications conglomerate. My favorite magazine became straight sales-garbage.

When it comes to knowledge, Larry's articles are as relevant to the antique outboarder as they ever were. Plus, Larry's writing is very entertaining.

For years, I nagged him to make a book of these articles. He finally gave in and gave me a lot of boxes of pretty well organized folders. I sorted and sifted through his original submissions and checked them against the published articles. Then I matched the pictures. Its wasn't as easy as it sounds, and took me nearly three years to get it as close to right as I am capable.

Three articles were missing, and the magazines were lost. A few selections are copies from the magazine. A few original pictures are missing, so they were copied from the magazine. Some corrections are visible from the original text. Even the fonts change. One thing is for sure, the knowledge remains.

In 1950 a major portion of the outboard industry was busily putting the finishing touches on its post war designs for introduction in 1951. Earlier in 1949, Mercury had unveiled its model KF-9 Thunderbolt, the worlds first production in-line four cylinder outboard and a super engine of its time. Further refinements and a model letter change, resulted in the KG-9 --a real screamer-- and this engine helped insure Keikhaufer Mercury almost total dominance in the field of outboard racing for years to come. Rated conservatively at 25 horsepower, the KG-9 was a direct drive engine having no neutral or reverse. Even the recoil starter was a dealer-installed option. Although the motor did not sell in large numbers, it was however, a milestone engine in outboarding history.

Johnson and Evinrude also marketed large engines in 1950. Johnson's PO-15 was a thirty-cubic-inch opposed twin, rated at 22 horsepower. Evinrude's Speedifour and Big Four were 50 and 60-inch four cylinder opposed engines that produced 33.4 and 50 horsepower respectively. These outboards however, were slight variations on designs that had originated in the 1930's. They were also basically military engines in that they had been strengthened to stand the rigors of combat service overseas, a task they performed admirably. Electric starting had been introduced to the outboarding public in 1930 but had proved unreliable, so in 1950 these engines were rope starting models only. They did not endear themselves to the boating public, nor were they intended to.

In 1951 Johnson and Evinrude introduced their thirty-six cubic inch alternate firing 25 h.p. top-of-the-line models. Except for engine shrouds and paint, the motors were identical and marked the beginning of what, in a few short years, would be a total marriage between the Johnson and Evinrude line of outboards.

Such companies as Martin, Champion, Scott-Atwater, Gale, Lauson, West Bend and others were also making valuable contributions to outboard technology and like the automotive industry, outboards were once again really getting off the ground in the post war boom.

With the exception of the Riley, a monstrous 75 h.p. five-cylinder radial outboard, which saw very limited production for a year or two, the largest engine up until 1957 was the 40 h.p. Mercury. 1957 saw the introduction of Mercury's first in-line six cylinder 60 h.p. motor. Johnson and Evinrude followed in 1958 with their 50 h.p. V-4's. During the '50's, Mercury rated their 40 h.p. models as being capable of 50 mph in stock form. For the most part, this was stretching things just a bit. Johnson and Evinrude simply stated 30-plus mph for their top of the line models. Even so, things sometimes got a little wild when a boating novice fired up a 60 h.p. Mark 75 on the transom of one of the then current crop of shallow Vee or round chine hulls. With horsepower increasing from year to year, outboard hulls became larger and heavier. Finally, with comfort and safety in mind, came the deep Vee hull.

Although horsepower has more than quadrupled since the 1950's speed has not increased all that much except for the super high performance rigs. Forty mph is still fast and a deep Vee hull needs a lot more power to push it around.

The point of all this nostalgia is not simply for its own sake, but to point out that a lot of fine outboards were built during the 1950's. Furthermore, a great many of them are still going strong and for an individual with limited resources and an urge to get out on the water, a 1950's outboard can provide a strong, reliable, and most important of all, an inexpensive means to such an end.

Generally speaking, marinas are unwilling to spend much time on these older engines. Two or three hours labor at current rates frequently exceeds the value of such an engine and that time can be more profitably spent servicing a current model. If a marina has a 25 to 35 h.p. OMC engine in good running condition, its price can run to $200 or more; an inflated value; but still a buy considering new outboard costs. However, if parts must be replaced, assuming the marina has them either from their old stock or from a parts engine, it is usually not worth the trouble from a business standpoint.

As a result, a great many fifties outboards, particularly the larger engines, are being sold for scrap or simply taken to the dump. I recently visited a local scrap metal dealer who had called me saying he recently cleaned out a nearby marina of about two dozen such unwanted engines and would I be interested in taking a look. The "pile" consisted of twenty or so OMC outboards of the 1950's and early '60's with a couple of Merc's and one Scott-Atwater thrown in for good measure. A closer inspection revealed that four or five of the OMC powerheads were in good shape with excellent compression and would probably run with little or no tinkering. These engines were being tossed because of problems from the powerhead down. Other motors of the same type illustrated definite powerhead trouble, but with good lower units, props, etc. It didn't take a trained outboard mechanic to realize that 3 or 4 good running engines could be put together simply by mating good powerheads with good lower units. Although I am basically interested in collecting and restoring outboards of a much older variety, I thanked the gentleman for the look-see. I didn't leave however, without buying a 35 h.p. Evinrude with an excellent powerhead for the sum of $8.00. One further note concerning scrapyards, is the fact that many of the smaller ones do not like to fool with outboards at all unless they own or have access to a "sweat-furnace" which is necessary for separating aluminium from iron and steel. Therefore, they are more than glad to turn these items over to anyone who wants them for a small price and indeed, many will not look side-ways at an old outboard.

Another source of inexpensive outboards of the older variety is of course the guy who owns one. And here I speak of the individual who has had an outboard sitting in the cellar or garage for years. It hasn't been used for a long time for any one of a number of reasons and the owner isn't sure it will even run. Chances are that he doesn't consider the engine of much value and if the truth be known, he would just like to get it out of the way.

The best way to reach this individual is to advertise. Many radio stations have swap and buy type programs on which the caller may state his wanted items or saleable wares over the air. In addition to this method there is always the classified section of the local newspaper plus those classified magazines that have become popular over the past few years. One note of caution, however. If you state that you are looking for a particular engine in good running condition, it is likely you will either get no response at all or you will locate someone who knows exactly what he has and thinks a great deal of his merchandise. This is the type of guy who would be willing to part with his outboard for a price which is usually too high.

A better way to locate your bargain engine is to advertise simply for old outboard motors and/or parts engines. Keeping in mind that many people do not know what kind of an outboard they have because they haven't had occasion to take a close look at it in sometime. It's impossible to tell what you're going to come up with and you should have a great deal more to choose from by way of people who just want to get an older piece of iron out from under foot.

One last note on advertising is as follows: if you call up over your local radio swap program for five straight days and come up with nothing; don't give up. On the sixth day you may be deluged with calls. In short, you never know who may be listening.

After coming up with an outboard of the type you were looking for and paying the bargain price you had in mind, there are a few points that should be touched upon. An owners or service manual. You probably didn't get one with the engine so your local marine dealer who handles this brand is your best bet. Most dealers will be glad to let you make copies of that material from their manuals which covers your engine. Although an OMC engine may be your best selection from a parts availability standpoint, you may end up with an outboard that hasn't been manufactured in 20 years. In this case, simply look in the yellow pages of an old phone book to find out who the dealer was at that time. Chances are that he is still in business but selling a current make. It is quite likely, however, that he has a pile of literature on your engine in his files. He may also have some common replacement parts such as a waterpump impeller, etc.

Probably the most common problem with an engine that hasn't been used in a number of years is gasoline that has been left in the tank, fuel lines, and carburetor for that period of time. After a year or two at the most, it is essential that these components be cleaned in order to avoid problems later on, even though the engine may start with the addition of fresh gas. Another item to check is the ignition points which should be filed and reset.

An occasional stuck piston ring can usually be freed by soaking with a little kerosene or gasoline additive. A more stubborn ring will almost always pop loose after the engine has been run a short time.

It should be noted here that the first thing to look for before purchasing an older outboard is whether it has decent compression. After checking to make sure the sparkplugs are in place, simply turn the engine over at a fairly rapid rate and feel the compression resistance in the cylinders. If the engine turns freely but has little or no compression, it would be best to look elsewhere or buy the engine for a few dollars for parts, if it is the type you are looking for.

An engine that is stuck and will not turn over should not necessarily be overlooked. Unless the motor has been left outside in the elements for years and is an obvious mess, the engine may be easily freed by soaking the rings through the spark plug holes and applying pressure to the flywheel directly. However, it should be stated to the owner that an outboard in this condition is not worth very much. The exception to this stuck engine rule is the motor that will turn a few degrees rotation and then meet with a definite hard resistance. This engine has major problems such as a broken connecting rod, crankshaft, etc. Forget it!

After having installed a new set of spark plugs of the correct heat range, you are ready to start your motor. Adjust the carburetor settings, check to see that the water pump is functioning and you're off.

For that fifties outboard in good running condition, you may finally be thinking in terms of restoring its appearance. Martin Seymour Paints (marketed through NAPA automotive parts stores) manufactures marine spray lacquer in spray cans in some of the old outboard colors such as Johnson green, Mercury green, and Evinrude blue. New decals are another story. A few dealers still have some. Most do not.

For the most part, outboards of the fifties are very much like those of today. True, advances have been made in breathing, economy, ignition and so on, but the fifties engine has its advantages also. It is a much simpler unit. Without the electronic this, and super sophisticated that, it lends itself very well to the weekend mechanic and part-time tinkerer with a manual in one hand, a few tools in the other, and a little common sense. Then too, we have the question of quality. Is the stamped-out plastic of today better than the die-cast aluminium of yesteryear? Who knows, but in this day of disposable everything, let's keep more of these older engines on the water.

Outboards of the Fifties
They're still with us!
BY LAWRENCE CARPENTER

Clockwise from left: Engines from the fifties (left to right) 1957 12-hp Buccaneer, 1956 30-hp Johnson, 1954 16-hp Merc, 1954 7½-hp Martin, 1952 25-hp Evinrude, and 1955 15-hp Evinrude. Parts interchangeability of OMC motors make them a wise choice. A 35 Evinrude powerhead purchased recently for eight dollars. Lower units of Evinrude Big Twin and Buccaneer will fit other OMC-built engines.

ANTIQUE CORNER

by

Lawrence C. Carpenter

Memories of Yesterday

"Come on", Mr. Haskill announced. "I bought that boat from Mr. Farnsworth last night at the church supper your mother and I went to. I mixed up some gas and I've got the old Johnson in the car. Let's go up and bring it down. You can get some breakfast when we get back."

John hadn't gotten up until almost 7:00. After all, it was Saturday. But John's dad was like that. Strictly spur-of-the-moment.

There it was, pulled up on the beach. It was a far cry from the Thompson they had used until last year, John thought, but then the Thompson had finally given up the ghost this spring and wasn't worth fixing. No sporty runabout was this, but it had been taken care of and certainly looked like it would float. That funny little steering wheel would be coming out, of course. It wouldn't be used that far forward with this motor.

"Not bad, huh?" John's dad remarked. John was about to indicate a somewhat reserved agreement when they were interrupted by Mr. Farnsworth's noisy approach.

The portly man in his early sixties dropped his burden on the beach in front of them.

"You might as well have these chair backs. They fit over

the seats. Just put 'em where you want. And here's a boat hook that goes with it. Sorry, there's no oars. Busted one about a month ago. The other one's in the boat."

Minutes later John and his dad were securing the trusty Johnson to the stern of the big rowboat. Mr. Haskill filled the gas tank about half full and replaced the cap.

"That ought to be plenty. We're only a mile or so downstream from here," he said.

"That's more motor than this things ever had", Mr. Farnsworth said. "Ought to go real good. I sold the old Elto to Reed Barnard at the hardware store in town. We sure ain't gonna need it or the boat in Arizona."

The boat drifted slowly away from shore as John wrapped the starting rope around the flywheel of the P-35.

"Choke it a couple times," his father yelled from shore as Mr. Farnsworth watched by his side. "She'll start right up."

The sun started to break through some low lying cloud cover that chilly early September morning in 1938. John watched as the float pin rose in the carburetor bowl and pushed it down a couple of times until gas dribbled out the hole. Let's see, choke lever down and spark a little beyond center. It was really nice to get back on the water, John thought as he yanked hard on the starter rope. The Johnson sputtered to life on the first pull.

A few years ago one Sunday afternoon, I found myself stumbling around amongst a bunch of old trunks and boxes in the dusty back room of an antique shop. I had questioned the proprietor a couple hours earlier about any old outboard or boat literature he might have lying around. After staring hard at the ceiling for a few moments the man had pointed toward a room at the rear of the shop.

"Seems to me I recall something," he said as I followed him through the door and into the cluttered room. "Some of this stuff has been here for years. You're welcome to take a look through it. Try not to spread it around to much."

I hadn't really found much except for two old photographs that had fallen out of an ancient world atlas when I knocked over a stack of books in the tight quarters. Oddly, the photos had fallen face up on the floor in the center of a shaft of sunlight coming through a dusty back window. After picking them up I looked through the atlas and then several other surrounding books to find any more pictures or maybe some clue as to the identity of these two. There was nothing.

Certainly the pictures hadn't seen the light of day for a good long time. The 5 x 7 photos were quite similar. The one included here is an enlargement centering on the boat itself and is the best of the pair. In the other picture the scene is somewhat the same, but the boat is headed almost straight away. The young man's head is turned to port and his profile can be seen. Also there is what looks to be young girl sitting in the forward seat facing the bow.

Your mind can wander after spending a few hours looking through piles of paper, at least mine does. As you know by now, none of the preceding story is actually true, however it somehow seemed indecent to allow these two anonymous pictures to face the future totally naked as it were. Some of the story comes from a deductive study of the details of the photos. Who knows, maybe its not that far off after all.

A.C. Postscript: An authentic decal or decal set completes and adds that final touch to any antique outboard restoration. Several members of the Antique Outboard Motor Club offer decals for one or more makes and models to other club members or anyone else for a nominal cost.

Decals, often colorful and intricate, are always costly in their duplication and production. Most often the reason for anyone reproducing a decal is that they need one themselves and of course decals are cheaper by the dozen. Repro decals are seldom a profit venture due to small demand. Many of those who make them available will not break even and most do not expect to.

The majority of decals available are for motors built just prior to WWI to those produced just after WWII though only a small percentage of makes and models are covered. Decals for outboards of the 1950's are almost non-existent at the present time and this brings me to the reason for all this.

Although fifties outboards are viewed as too new by many antique outboarders, interest in many models has increased in recent years. Cosmetically speaking, some paints are still available and some others can be closely matched, but decals are a stumbling block.

   Some current dealers undoubtably still have N.O.S. fifties decals tucked away somewhere. Many have been tossed out over the years and more certainly will be. However, anyone having some of these relics might consider donating them to the Antique Outboard Motor Club to be made available through the AOMC Store to those interested in them for a small charge. Although many of these decals for motors of the fifties or older are probably unusable because of age deterioration some may still be saved or more importantly be used as patterns for repros by a member or even the club itself. Incidently, the AOMC is a registered non-profit organization. Engine or even auxillary tank decals would be gratefully received and may be sent to Sam Vance, AOMC Store, RD2, Box 33C, Unadilla, NY 13849.

The Outboard and its Early Days

With a new decade upon us and outboard motors topping the 300 HP mark I think more than a few boating enthusiasts are still in a state of shock after contemplating what has become of their favorite means of marine power in so short a period of time. Indeed, at a time when almost all forms of transportational power are being sized downward, de-emphasized, detuned or downright ignored, not so with the outboard motor. Perhaps in no other field has the internal combustion engine seem more technological development than in the outboard.

It has been over two decades since an outboard cracked the 100 MPH barrier. In this day and age of fast moving technical advancement, twenty years is a lifetime, so I think it is reasonable to predict that the day is not far off when an outboard motor may well hold the world's speed record for propeller driven craft and in so doing, come to dominate the field of unlimited hydroplane racing. Furthermore, with the recent introduction of the current crop of really big mills and their excellent power to weight ratio it is only a matter of time before one or more find their way into the chassis of Formula 1 or Indianapolis type race cars. But before we contemplate these and other developments of the 1980s and beyond lets take a look at the outboard motor's family tree and examine a few twists that its taken over the years.

The middle to late 1800s saw the introduction of a variety of weird contraptions to the boating scene. Although the majority never saw a drop of water, but remained in a patent office file or in the mind of a boating enthusiast, it was indeed a time of great inventive creativity and as all forms of transportation were in their infancy the outboard too found its beginning. The first device of a truly outboard nature was patented by Thomas Reece of Philadelphia in 1866. This was a hand crank unit and except that it used a drive shaft and bevel gears instead of a chain it looked very much like the wooden hand crank model pictured in this article. The first outboard motors utilized electric power and the first of these was introduced in 1881 at the Paris Exposition by Gustave Trouve. Picture if you will the wooden hand unit in the photo complete with

1

chain drive, but with an electric motor in place of the horizontal crank member and you have an accurate recreation of this outboard. Unfortunately these early efforts were never marketed.

The first gasoline engine powered outboards arrived during the late 1890s. American Motor Co., (not to be confused with the modern auto manufacturer) produced a handful of crude single cylinder outboards in 1896. In the period up until 1909 several more companies entered the field and the idea of detachable and portable marine power began to take hold in the public eye. Perhaps the most significant of these firms was that of Cameron B. Waterman who introduced his Waterman "Porto" engine in 1906 and began production in quantity. It was indeed Waterman who coined the term "outboard", although the name "rowboat motor" persisted well into the twenties due largely to the fact that it denoted the only real practical use of these small, low rpm engines.

In 1909 the first Evinrude rowboat motor was sold. Although born in Norway, Ole Evinrude was raised in the farm country of Wisconsin. Evinrude never considered himself suited to farm life and so as a teenager left home to work in a machine shop. At age 30 Evinrude had educated himself through various jobs and much study to the point where he was an expert machinist, tool maker and pattern maker. Moreover, his new bride, Bess proved to have a keen business sense. The Evinrude Motor Co. grew quickly to a point of leadership in the young outboard industry.

As with any successful venture, long hours day after day plus frequent moves to larger quarters can exert considerable physical strain and such was the case with Bess Evinrude who had run the business end of the company from the beginning. Ole, therefore decided to sell out following the 1913 season to take life easy with Bess and their son Ralph in an active yet relaxed retirement. Such was the reputation of the Evinrudes that upon selling the company Ole agreed not to enter the field of outboard motor manufacture for five years, thereby affording the buyer a feeling of safety from the immediate competition should Evinrude start another company.

2

During the teens many more companies joined the industry. With the outboard motor an established fact, the accent came to fall on features which promised ease of starting and handling. Features such as the variable pitch propeller, the flywheel magneto, and underwater exhaust made their appearance. Caille, Lockwood-Ash, Ferro, Koban, Wright, Federal, Spinaway, Joymotor, and others became familiar names in the pages of sport and boating magazines. For the first time the boating public had a reliable source of portable power that could be afforded by a larger number of people. Although not inexpensive; the average price ranging from 75-100 dollars, the outboard or rowboat motor brought power boating out of the yacht clubs and social circles of the well to do and gave it to the guy next door who simply wanted to power a rental boat during his vacation.

The list of manufacturers was perhaps at its greatest during the teens. Like the auto industry, the field of outboards was wide open and many companies wanted to share in the profits of an ever expanding market. Some firms lasted only a year or two. Others tried their hand at it for a while and then went back to their mainstay such as stationary or inboard power plants. A great many, however, prospered for a generation before the industry settled itself down to several large and prosperous companies. Of all the makers of that period, only Evinrude survives today.

The year 1920 saw basically the same outboard that had been around for six or eight years. Even though many features had been added, engine technology of the period had pretty much stayed the same. The average outboard had a single cylinder, produced two or three horsepower at 600 to 1000 rpm and was constructed mainly of cast iron, bronze and brass. World War I however, gave a quick shot in the arm to the internal combustion engine. Engines produced for aircraft, land transportation, and marine use both here and abroad showed great strides in design and the use of lighter metals, notably aluminum. These advances coupled with the progress of the companies themselves was to change the outboard motor drastically during the 1920s.

During the last year of the war about the time that his five year agreement was up, Ole Evinrude was working on another outboard motor. Retirement and relaxation were fine, but as far as the Evinrudes were concerned it was time to get back to work. Ole's new engine was a light weight opposed twin cylinder using liberal amounts of aluminum for the lower unit, tower housing, rudder, etc. Although the opposed twin had been tried before, it had been heavy and cumbersome, but with his higher revving design Ole knew he had a winner. In the two cycle layout both cylinders fired at once thereby eliminating the vibration of the unbalanced singles. While developing only 3 HP it was evident that this design would permit much larger engines to be built.

The Evinrudes, of course, took the engine to their old company, Evinrude Motor Co., so they might have the opportunity to manufacture it. Surprisingly, however, Evinrude Motor Co. was not interested, as they were doing quite well building essentially the same motor they had before the war. They could see no reason to spend money to produce an entirely different model.

Rather than try to interest another concern in their motor the Evinrudes decided to start their own company once more. Gathering friends and relatives together with the Evinrudes' small amount of capital, the Elto Company was formed. The name, incidentally was born of Bess' merchandising genius. She simply took the first letters of the words Evinrude Light Twin Outboard. On the nameplate of all Elto outboards was inscribed "Designed by Ole Evinrude". The first Eltos hit the market in the spring of 1921 and were instant favorites of the boating public.

The Johnson brothers, Lou, Harry and Clarence gained their substantial mechanical and engineering expertise through a variety of accomplishments during their younger days in Indiana. The Johnsons built and successfully flew the first monoplane in America in 1911. Their marine engines powered some of the fastest racing boats of that time. Their main business venture, however, was the production of bicycle engines during the late teens. Not lucky enough to have a Bess Evinrude in the family, the Johnsons relied heavily on Warren Ripple, and enterprising businessman, to run the

4

company while they guided the technical aspects of the product. The bicycle engine was a small two cycle, air cooled, opposed twin of 1-1/2 HP, but the availability of inexpensive automobiles and motorcycles cut deeply into their market. For this reason, and also because their first love had always been the water, the Johnson brothers entered the outboard field. Late in December on 1921 the first Johnson engines were shipped from the South Bend, Indiana plant. The motor was basically a water cooled version of the bicycle engine producing 2 HP. It was smooth running, easy to operate, and weighed only 33 pounds. The pubic loved it.

In the early to mid twenties the opposed twin cylinder configuration gained rapid acceptance as the only way to go although earlier designs were still being built for those who preferred them. Other companies were not exactly standing still. Caille and Lockwood-Ash had large followings and indeed built fine engines.

Until 1925 the outboard was generally a small machine suitable for fishing or a leisurely cruise aboard the family rowboat, but the image was about to change and change drastically. In 1925 Johnson Motor Company tested its Big Twin. This 22 cu. in. opposed twin rated at 6 HP was the first production outboard to propel a boat up out of the water and on a firm planing attitude. It established a world outboard speed record of slightly better than 16 MPH. Other companies brought out their higher powered models and the race was on. The end of 1926 saw the speed record almost doubled and by the close of the decade 60 cu. in. opposed four cylinder monsters were screaming across the water at nearly 50 MPH. The period from 1925 to 1930 must be referred to as the outboard motor's golden age in that never in its history, before or since, had the outboard been so popular. Outboard motors and their feats were a genuine news item. Outboard racing must certainly have begun years before when two or more like minded individuals found themselves together on the same pond, but now it seemed everyone was getting into the act. A race could be found on any weekend anywhere there was water and the events ranged from wild free-for-alls to finally somewhat more orderly affairs as any one of a number of early regulatory bodies realized that some general rules were needed to avoid the utter chaos that often resulted. Outboard advertising was likely to appear in almost any newspaper or magazine although was naturally concentrated in sporting and boating publications. Companies fought each other tooth and nail for the latest marathon win or the latest speed record which might be broken anyway in some other part of the country the next day. Top outboard racers of the time became as well known as major league ball players.

Outboard hulls themselves took on strange shapes as they strove to keep pace with higher powered engines. Some engine manufacturers such as Johnson built their own line of boats and marketed specific engine and hull combinations. Years earlier outboards had been clamped onto anything available, sometimes in a very makeshift manner. Now hulls were being tailored to the sport.

The shallow vee and flat bottomed hulls planed the easiest. The single stepped hydroplane hull lessened the wetted surface for higher speeds and this feature was incorporated into the bottom of many slim runabout designs.

The outboard reached out for any and all challenges. The New York to Miami run was accomplished time and again using the larger engines coupled to lightweight hulls with frames and stringers about as thick as a baby's wrist.

In March of 1929 Outboard Motor Corporation (OMC) was formed from the merger of three successful companies; Elto, Evinrude and Lockwood. Ole Evinrude was named president. The Lockwood line of motors had to be dropped early in the depression that followed the stock market crash and the outboard industry as a whole took a giant backward step as did the entire country. Johnson Motor Co. was particularly hard hit in that they had been set for a big push when economic misfortune came. Although the company continued it did not ever really recover and so, it too was purchased by Outboard Motor Corp. in 1935 making OMC the world's largest maker of outboards.

Though not from a sales standpoint, 1930 was a bright year for new outboard features. Electric starting appeared on the larger models of five separate brands and Johnson brought out its line of alternate firing twins although it continued to build an opposed engine model until 1950. After recovering from the depression the mid to late 1930s proved to be a period of refinement for the industry as a whole.

In February of 1942 outboard production for the public market was stopped by federal order, however the industry was far from idle and indeed contributed heavily toward the war effort. Outboards of every size were built for the military and were used around the world. From crossing the Rhine in Germany to assaulting a Japanese held island in the Pacific, or simply the lightweight engine a downed airman found rolled up in his life raft; the outboard motor performed admirably. And the industry found other ways to serve the country. Its manufacturing and engineering capabilities produced parts that found their way into all types of military hardware. Mercury for instance, a relative newcomer to the field, built vast quantities of engines that powered target and drone aircraft. Evinrude and Johnson's larger engines were used to power pumps aboard ships and the record shows that more than one heavily damaged vessel managed to stay afloat through their use.

The end of World War II and the beginning of the 1950s brought the outboard to a point that was easily recognized by most of the boating public. Indeed today many of these older engines are still in use. However, engines of the teens, twenties, and thirties; although not very visible are still around and in large numbers.

An item such as an old car or boat that had been lying around to become an unsightly object in the yard has generally long since gone to the scrap heap. Not so with an old outboard. Though many have and continue top go in this direction, thousands of old motors, being relatively small items, have been stuffed away in attics, cellars, sheds, etc. where they remain all but forgotten. This plus the fact that interest in old outboards is almost non-existent support the low value of these motors now or in the foreseeable future. They, therefore, present an easily affordable hobby for those few

7

who love old engines. By nature of their age, their sometimes odd engineering features, and their surprising performance, they offer a fascinating avocation to anyone who has an interest in outboard powered boats.

There is one organization in the country made up of old outboard enthusiasts. It is the Antique Outboard Motor Club Inc. The club publishes a quarterly magazine and a monthly newsletter and for annual dues of $12.00, is open to anyone who is interested. For further information one can write the membership chairman, Walter Verner, 4304 Harding Rd. Nashville, TN 37205

For those interested in reading further about the history of the outboard there is but one comprehensive book that I know of, it is the Pictorial History of Outboard Motors by J. W. Webb with Robert W. Carrick and is published by Renaissance Editions Inc. of New York. Mr. Webb incidentally was a long time friend and associate of the Evinrudes and so much material is from first hand experience.

Left to right: A flywheel magneto was introduced on the 1914 Evinrude. The 1915 Gray Gearless eliminated the geared lower unit. 1921 Lockwood Ash is still a strong runner.

OUTBOARD SPOTLIGHT

1916 Evinrude Four Cycle Twin Model "AA"

Specifications

Bore & Stroke	2¼ x 2½
Cubic Inches	19.87
Horsepower	4 @700-900 RPM
Weight	90 lbs
Price	$125.00

Although the forerunner of successfull Evinrude opposed twin cylinder designs, the 1916 Model "AA" was not a favorite with the ever expanding outboard buying public of the day. The engine was heavy, cumbersome, expensive and oftentimes difficult to run. During its brief production from 1916 to mid 1917, 1399 motors were manufactured which did not compare favorably to production figures of Evinrude's standard single cylinder, two cycle outboard in its many forms.

The Model "AA" did not utilize a separate oil sump, but rather the gas-oil mix of a standard two cycle. A fresh charge of gas from the four ball Kingston carburetor was sucked into the crankcase where it received the necessary oomph to be shoved out and into a foot long manifold passage that ended with a vacuum operated valve in the cylinder head. Exhause was by way of a cam operated valve, through an exhause manifold and into the almost prohibitively restrictive muffler system. Restrictive that is, unless the two exhaust cutouts were opened in which case the muffler did little or nothing in abating the racket which then ensued. Although nearly all outboards of the day exhibited poor breathing characteristics, the Evinrude Model "AA" carried this trait to extremes thereby contributing greatly to its operating difficulties.

Although Evinrude had introduced the flywheel magneto only two years before in 1914 these mags as on the Model "AA" were suprisingly efficiant. The engine pictured here carries an accessory wiring harness and switch that allows a 1½ volt dry cell to be hooked into the system to assist in cold or damp weather starts if necessary.

The Model "AA" was equipped with what was called automatic reverse, a feature of the standard model "a" and other Evinrude models for over a decade. A twisting motion of the tiller handle allowed the torque of the rotating propeller to turn the entire lower unit and tower housing 180 degrees into a locked reverse position. Forward speed was resumed in the same manner by allowing the lower unit to complete its 360 degree circle to normal position. Although viewed today as an odd and clumsy approach to a simple problem this system worked quite well at a time long before gearshifts when these lower units were using bearings of bronze against bronze.

Admittedly, the Model "AA" had its drawbacks. It was, however, an outboard of supreme quality in workmanship and appearance, being as it was the top of the Evinrude line in a highly competitive market populated by many more manufacturers than exist today. The model "AA" remains a very striking piece of equipment. Polished brass, bronze, and nickel plate make up at least one third of the surface area with the remainder painted a medium gray, the shade of which corresponds closely with industrial or universal gray on current paint charts.

Production of the "AA" ceased in 1917, but in 1923 the same basic engine reappeared in two cycle form. In 1927 this motor evolved into the Evinrude Speeditwin, a model which was produced until 1950. One of Evinrude's most productive model series in its history, the Speeditwin set countless speed and endurance records in class "C" racing and performed admirably during World War II as a military outboard.

The engine pictured here is serial number 53823. It was restored from an excellent original and is from the Carpenter Collection.

THAT FIRST BOAT

(full length article for TBM in July 1981 not an Antique Corner column)

When asked, a great many people can fondly recall their first car, their first date, and perhaps their first ride in an airplane. But for those who love the water and the craft that ride thereon, we must add one more the list : That First Boat

The year was 1951. I was eleven, and we did not have a boat. At that age, in my particular circumstances I had become increasingly appalled with this fact,

"We live on the lake," I would remind my parents, "We even have a dock."

I realized later that my parent's basic interests did not rise and fall with the crystal clear waters of Lake Winnipesaukee. However, during the long hot New Hampshire summers of that period I spent a great many hours in and around the water. In my young estimation a boat of some kind was crucial to my very existence and I was determined to press forward to this end.

"We used to have a boat." My father would say.

I had heard this all before. One day during the fall of 1938 my dad had arrived home having just come off duty as a motorcycle police officer with the NH State Police. This was during the tail end of the famous hurricane of that year that devastated much of the Northeast and in our area the landscape had taken quite a beating. One quick look down by the shore revealed my father's small 16 foot mahogany speedboat smashed and broken and laying on the rocky bottom half out of the water. My dad would relate how he had stripped all the hardware from the Laconia hull and then removed and completely dismantled the four cylinder Van Blerk Junior engine which now resided in several boxes in his machine shop in the garage. After this bit of nostalgia I would remind my father that I did not exist in 1938 and that I hadn't had the benefit of this or any other boat.

After a discussion with my parents concerning my ability to swim, the responsibility of having a boat and my willingness to use it at their direction, it was agreed that I could "look around" the area to see what might be available. Keep in mind that the pleasure boating industry in those days was not what it is now and while new boats were of course available, my first craft would be in the form of a used wooden rowboat.

At age eleven I was not totally without funds. My summer job consisted of catching crawfish for a local bait shop that sold them to vacationing fishermen who in turn dangled them before a large smallmouth bass population. Two or three evenings a week I would set forth along the shoreline after dark with my flashlight and pail in search of these swift little creatures as they ventured out from their daylight hiding places. A catch of two or three hundred a night was not uncommon and I received two cents apiece. When as a teenager a few years later earning seventy-five cents an hour after school I recall looking back at my crawfish job and two to four dollars an hour with amazement though at the time I hadn't given it much thought. So when looking for my first boat I considered myself a serious buyer with cash in hand, a feeling which I am sure any eleven year old of today would enjoy as much as I did then.

The first boat I happened upon that looked like it might be available was located only a few houses down the lake. It was upside down beside a camp and hadn't been used in a couple seasons. It was about eight feet long, of the punkinseed variety, and had obviously been built from some plans that appeared in Popular Mechanics or a similar publication. It was beautiful and the owner said he would let it go for ten dollars. The next day when I got my parents to look at it they wasted no time in voicing their disapproval.

"It is much too small and it certainly doesn't look safe." My mother stated. Those were her sentiments in a nutshell. While fastening me with a stern gaze my father observed that the boat could not be rowed, but needed an outboard motor to push it around.

This fact had not escaped me but I just looked at him and said "Oh?"

"Keep on looking." was their combined verdict.

Early the following Saturday my father remarked at breakfast that he had heard of a boat for sale a short distance up the lake and why didn't I bike up and take a look at it. I paused only long enough to get the name and directions.

I arrived at the described camp and knocked at the door. The older looking man said he was Mr. MacCalister and seemed to already know who I was and why I was there.

"I'll show you what I've got," he said and led me the way down to the small beach where there were three or four rowboats in and out of the water. "Well, here she is," he said, indicating by far the largest of the lot. "What do you think?"

After picturing the previous boat in my mind this thing looked like an ark. It must be at least fifteen feet long, I thought. Although of questionable heritage, it did have nice lines. The gunwales flared from the three foot transom to a generously wide beam and on forward, ending at the straight stem which jutted ahead at an appropriate angle. Two continuous pine planks, the upper slightly over lapping the lower formed each side of the hull and the bottom was cross planked in the conventional flat bottomed manner. A gentle sway of the outboard keel suggested both transom and stem would be just out of water with the boat at rest and unloaded. Seating was of the standard type layout except there were four instead of the usual three because of her large size.

"She's been around for a while, but she's solid," Mr. MacCalister offered. "Paint should hold for this season at least and the oar locks and oars go with her."

I had been walking in and around the boat to get the view from every angle. I was beginning to appreciate the possibilities that went with a big boat.

"She's good sized, isn't she?" I said, answering his comments.

"She is that, but you'll find she pulls easy and you won't have to worry if you're out and the wind kicks up".

I nodded agreement.

"Say, why don't you just load your bicycle in there forward and row on back and see what your parents have to say?"

I quickly agreed this was a fine idea.

In no time the bike was loaded and I was in place as Mr. MacCalister had instructed waiting for him to shove me off. After assuring me the boat was soaked and tight I was on my own.

I was amazed how easily the boat glided along and I formulated detailed plans on the way home. Dozens of times in the early morning I had seen an old laker chugging quietly along down the lake with the old man at the helm trolling for trout or salmon. This was a common sight going back as far as I could remember which at the time had to be at least five or six years; but the point was that this laker had a forward enclosure fabricated of canvas over curved metal or wooden bows. I could already visualize such a setup ahead of me as I rowed. I was going to have a cabin cruiser.

As I neared our dock I happened to take a closer look at the transom. There in plain view were the two small round indentations in the wood giving testimony to the fact that there had been an outboard motor on my boat.

My mother and dad fully approved of my choice in boats and quite frankly it was hard to believe there had been a time when I thought I could get along with something smaller. Right about then I was shocked to recall that I had never even asked the price. When I mentioned this fact to my father he didn't seem as concerned as I thought he was going to be, but simply said he somehow recalled the figure of twenty dollars and that he would pay Mr. MacCalister a visit. I just looked at my parents and was getting ready to say something when my mother smiled and said. "Lets just say you don't have to bring it back. " I am somewhat embarrassed to admit that it was some years later that it dawned on me that in all probability my parents had orchestrated most of the events surrounding my final acquisition of a boat.

After rejoicing in my own good fortune and admiring my new boat for the next hour or so I began to formalize the next step in my plan. Shortly before noon I watched as my father left his garage/shop and headed up to the house. A minute or two later I followed.

"I have a great idea," I announced to them both. "Why don't we pack a picnic lunch and go across the lake to the beach?" There were no camps or homes across the lake. For a five mile stretch the Boston & Maine Railroad tracks hugged the shoreline with just an occasional bit of real estate sticking out into the water. A hundred years previous when the tracks had been laid the term "shore property" bore no significance whatever and indeed in 1951 it didn't mean much more. Most of the land behind the tracks was owned by the state of New Hampshire. In short the land on the other side of the lake was wilderness and included three or four small beaches which were used occasionally by anyone who cared to and who had a boat to get there. My parents

4

knew the area quite well from several years past, mostly pre-1938, but I had been an infrequent visitor though not by choice and only with friends of the family with a boat, and a power boat at that.

"Do you know how far that is?" my father asked. Do you feel like rowing all the way over there?"

The other side of the lake was nearly a mile straight across and I did indeed have an idea how log it would take. "I'll row." I said eagerly.

My father just nodded slowly and glanced briefly at my mother. "Of course, it would be a lot faster if you had an outboard motor."

I couldn't believe what I was hearing. This had been much easier than I had though and hastily mumbled agreement.

"I wouldn't recommend anything too large." My father continued. "Even a five or six horse with that bottom will stick the bow way up in the air with just one person aboard."

I was certainly ready to accept a smaller engine, in fact, any engine at all. It was agreed that after a conventional lunch at home we would go out looking for an outboard motor.

Jerry's Sporting Goods Store was located a couple miles down the road and seemed a logical place to start looking. While not a marina, Jerry Lapointe did carry the line of Martin outboards plus a few used motors. With my limited finances in mind our attention came to rest on an ancient looking little engine in the corner. Jerry stated that he had recently taken the engine in trade and although he didn't know much about it, it did seem to run well and appeared to be in good shape for its age, which he and my father placed at somewhere between twenty and thirty years. As we brought it out for a closer look the words Johnson Motor Co. in raised letters were clearly visible on the exposed flywheel rope plate. Underneath where it said model number was stamped AB-25 and near that was a serial number.

My father explained to me that the motor was an opposed twin cylinder and commented that the entire lower part of the outboard seemed to be made of brass or bronze. A consensus of opinion of everyone in the store placed its' horsepower at about three.

The priced turned out to be the same as the boat - twenty dollars. We took the little outboard home.

Although sometimes difficult to start, after being thoroughly briefed on the motors operation, I was cruising around our immediate section of the lake that very afternoon. My father had warned me several times at keeping my hands away from the flywheel with the motor running, but I will always believe that he let me find out about not touching the spark plug for myself.

The following weekend when I went to the garage to get the motor I was shocked to find that my father had taken it apart.

"Hop in the car," he said. "We're going to get this flywheel charged."

Not having the faintest idea what he meant, I did as I was told and on the way he explained that the engine would probably start much easier once this was done.

At the boat yard a man my dad knew as Mr. Cannon placed the flywheel on a machine of some kind and connected a few wires. When he pressed a switch a loud buzzing sound came from the machine for a few seconds until he released the switch. I couldn't see where anything had been done or that it would make any difference, but it sure did. Once back together the engine started so easily it was almost comical. We really didn't need the starting rope as the motor could be started by simply rocking the flywheel past compression with your hand. At every and any opportunity I was proud to show anyone who was interested how easy my outboard would start.

For the next few weeks that summer the boat saw constant use. Picnics across the lake and family trips of several miles were undertaken on weekends. However, most of its use was that of my own invention, the majority of this being in the immediate neighborhood with summer friends.

Almost imperceptibly at first and then with alarming certainty my outboard motor was losing power. After quelling not a small amount of panic, I methodically attacked the problem. I cleaned and reset the spark plugs and readjusted the carburetor as my father had described when we got the motor. No luck and the ailment worsened. I sought out my dad in the depths of his machine shop and laid the situation at his feet in the form of an extreme emergency.

At the moment my father was unimpressed. It seemed that he was in the process of setting up an important job and the best he could do was give my problem some thought, at least for the present.

During the next couple days the performance of the motor deteriorated to a slow troll, but seemed to hold at that level and chug along smoothly. By the following weekend I had become resigned to the fact that my outboard had putted its last putt. However when I returned from an early morning fishing trip at a nearby cove my father was waiting on the dock.

"Let's take a look at that thing," he said simply.

Once perched on a wooden stand in front of the shop door my dad inspected the old engine as he moved this and adjusted that. I stood close by, but said nothing, hoping that he somehow could perform the necessary miracle. Finally he wrapped the starting rope around the flywheel and holding the engine steady with one hand, gave a mighty pull with the other. The motor chugged into life and then BANG! The engine literally screamed as it turned up faster than it was ever meant to. My father quickly reached for the mag cutout switch and held on until finally there was silence.

The loud bang had startled us both and I found myself sitting on the ground. Close by was the remains of the motor's muffler can which had been blown right off the exhaust manifolds. My dad picked up the almost flat piece of sheet metal and chuckled. One side was thickly caked with black carbon and dad explained that the exhaust holes in the muffler had become plugged and the motor was choking on its own exhaust fumes.

In a little more than an hour the little Johnson was sporting a new exhaust system. Dad had sawed off both the exhaust manifold midway between the cylinders and the muffler caps and plugged the ends. He then bored a one inch hole in each of the undersides of the manifolds and inserted lengths of steel electrical conduit in the holes for exhaust pipes. A cross bracket bolted to the cavitation plate anchored the bottom ends of pipes which were cut at an angle to help allow the exhaust gasses to escape underwater.

7

The engine ran quieter and with more power than it ever had. I quickly found that the dual exhaust made a nice throaty sound not unlike that of an inboard and I would sometimes ride up amidships where a slight wave action would lift the exhaust out of the water occasionally.

The Johnson continued to run perfectly, but the following season it was placed in semi-retirement in favor of a faster five HP Flambeau. Therein started a progressive chain of boats and motors which has continued to this day, however that first boat will always be remembered with a special fondness.

I am sorry to say that the original boat has long since gone the way of most other wooden rowboats of that time period, but the little Johnson AB-25, though it has not run in many years, remains alive and well on a stand in my cellar.

On several occasions over the years my father and I argued, mostly in jest, about exactly who owns the engine. We both agree that the price of the boat and motor was twenty dollars each and we also agree that we each paid for one item, but probably because only the outboard still exists we each recall that we paid for the motor. As I say, these discussions are really unimportant except for the fun they provide because my dad and I will readily confess that it doesn't really matter which one of us bought it.

I have yet to restore the Johnson although recalling the events written here I think it will be soon. Possibly because as a child I wanted every new outboard I saw I now have about three hundred such engines dating from the 1950s back to the early 1900s. Though I have restored many of these relics I had put off the AB-25 until I ran across the parts to restore the exhaust system to original specifications, but the more I think about it the more I think I'll restore the outboard and leave the exhaust the way my father built it. I would really like to hear that special sound again.

1930 Johnson Model J-25

In 1925 if you were looking for a small, easily portable and dependable trolling motor you might have settled on the newly introduced Johnson model J-25. Late in 1921 Johnson had commenced shipment of its first outboard, the model "A", an ultra light opposed twin of 2 HP weighing 35 lbs. This engine along with the first model of Ole Evinrude's newly organized "Elto" company revolutionized the outboard industry almost overnight toward the concept of more compact designs promising higher power and away from the heavy slugging singles of the teens.

Available with its own specially designed canoe bracket, the model "A" (referred to later as the Johnson Water-Bug) gained wide acceptance as a truly portable fishing motor. The J-25 took this idea a step further, or rather smaller.

An efficient flywheel magneto supplied spark to the single cylinder engine as fed through Johnson's own float feed carburetor. Starting was accomplished by winding the starter cord around the rope plate atop the flywheel. The healthy bark of the small mill was quieted by a cast aluminum muffler located along side the block, one of the last engines to use this method as underwater exhaust was gaining wide acceptance during this period. Cooling the cast iron powerhead was handled by an externally mounted piston water pump. The motor featured 360 degree pivoting for maneuvering in close quarters and included a handy carrying handle incorporated into the tiller bracket. In operation, the J-25 was not unlike a comparable sized outboards of today except for its separate spark and gas controls.

The motor was finished almost entirely in metal brightwork. The cylinder was cadmium plated, the tower housing nickel plated and the remainder, aluminum castings or polished aluminum.

The J-25 was built from 1925 to 1932 and during these years remained basically unchanged. Price actually decreased during this time period from $125 to $115 and comparable models a few years later were in the 50 to 60 dollar range.

Specifications

Bore & Stroke	2" x 2-1/2"
Cubic Inches	4.71
Horsepower	1-1/2 @ 2700 RPM
Weight	27 lbs.
Price	$115.00

1954 MERCURY MARK 20

Faster than a scalded cat, able to win more races in a single season. To the second statement, most certainly, to the first; well maybe, maybe not. This must be regarded as a gray area because here we lack the pertinent information regarding this particular feline. Well enough of this foolishness, the fact is that the outboard was a Merc and such was the reputation Mercury enjoyed back in the late forties and nineteen fifties and to some degree still does to this day. The word was that a Merc would usually skin the competition alive whether on the race course or the family runabout. There were several reasons for this. First of all, Mercury launched a serious program shortly after WWII. OMC (Johnson & Evinrude) did not. Outboard racing classes "J" though "D" came to be dominated by Mercury although several drivers chose to stick with their prewar OMC racing engines and a few did quite well, particularly in class "C" where Mercury didn't field a 30 cu. in. motor until 1956. Class "F" similarly was populated mainly Evinrude 4-60s until the introduction of Mercury's 6 cylinder Mark 75-H in 1957. Not that the 4-60's were dogs, but they were a dying breed and parts were often hard to come by. In short, with the exception of a couple other outboard makers who from time to time gave the Mercs a run for their money in Class "B", the outboard racing game in those days was basically a Kiekhaefer Mercury institution.

Secondly we come to the rating of horsepower. A case in point: In 1947-49 Mercury's Model KE4 produced 7-1/2 HP from 11 cu. in. and was a solid, well designed engine. Performance wise it was closely in tune with competitive engines and few shrieks of protest were heard. But shortly thereafter the Model KG-4 was introduced. It looked almost identical to its predecessor but under its integrally mounted gas tank resided a completely redesigned powerhead of almost 15 cu. in. conveniently just under the class "A" limit. The horsepower rating? Again 7-1/2. Referred to as the "baby hurricane", the KG-4 would outrun any other stock 10 HP outboard and then some. In racing trim it became the KG-4H and literally took over class "A". Incidentally these engines are still competitive today! Therein grew the Mercury legend; speed.

However this growing reputation did not always pay off in sales. In 1951 Mercury offered its Model KG-9 rated at 25 HP, but producing close to 40 in the language of Johnson or Evinrude's 25 HP top of the line models. For top speed on the family runabout there was no contest, although in engine versatility there was no comparison. The Merc was a direct drive, forward speed engine only. Johnson and Evinrude were equipped with a full gearshift of forward, neutral, and reverse. A very handy feature at dockside, the Merc, although well designed and quality built, like any temperamental pussycat, could be quite finicky in the inexperienced clutches of the average boater. The OMC 25's on the other hand possessed few, if any discernible vices and would purr for almost anyone. The KG-9Hs came to dominate class "D" but sold in limited numbers to the general public. The OMC 25s entered only a "Sunday Boaters" special 36 cu. in. class created especially for them, but sold engines by the thousands. The whole situation was not taken lightly by those involved. In those years of rigid and faithful product loyalty, (remember the Ford and Chevy owners of the fifties?), discussions at the local outboard dealership while airing the pros and cons of the current models sometimes developed into physical violence.

Space here does not allow a thorough going over of the whys and wherefores of the "Great Outboard Horsepower Controversy" of the late forties and early fifties, however let it suffice for now to say that by 1954 the dust has somewhat settled. The Mark 40 rated at 25 HP suddenly evolved into the Mark 50 rated at 40. The KG-4 rated at 7-1/2 HP became the Mark 15 listed at 10 HP and the KH-7 originally quoted at 10 HP was transformed into the Mark 20 banging out a solid 16. All this with little or no engine modifications but with much needed features such as a full gear shift. The cat became by no means tame, but just a little more sophisticated and for those who required their meat raw, there was still the racing models. One final comment on the care and feeding of the Mercury legend of speed. During most of the past three decades Mercury has built larger outboards than the competition.

The Mark 20 pictured here was one of the new breed of Mercurys. An engine of supreme quality and durability, the Mark 20 is in this writer's opinion perhaps the most ascetically beautiful outboard ever produced. A great many survive today and a large number are still running strong; but for those who own them the parts availability situation is somewhat dismal and for the most part is limited to another Mark 20. It is possible that your dealer may have a part or two tucked away if he has been in business for a long time, however, you may have better luck at your local NAPA Auto Parts store. NAPA publishes a catalog of parts for outboard motors which lists such items as water pump impellers, carburetor and ignition parts for this engine as well as parts for other older outboards. NAPA also carries the old Mercury green paint in spray cans under the Martin Seymour label. A nice thing about cosmetically restoring the "20" and many other of the old green Mercs is that there are no hard to find decals to replace. So if you have one of the old Mark 20's, treat her kindly. There's probably a lot of life left in the old cat yet.

1954 MERCURY MARK 20
SPECIFICATIONS

Bore & Stroke	2-7/16 x 2-1/8
Cubic Inches	19.8
Horsepower	16 @ 4000 RPM
Weight	73 lbs
Price	$343.50

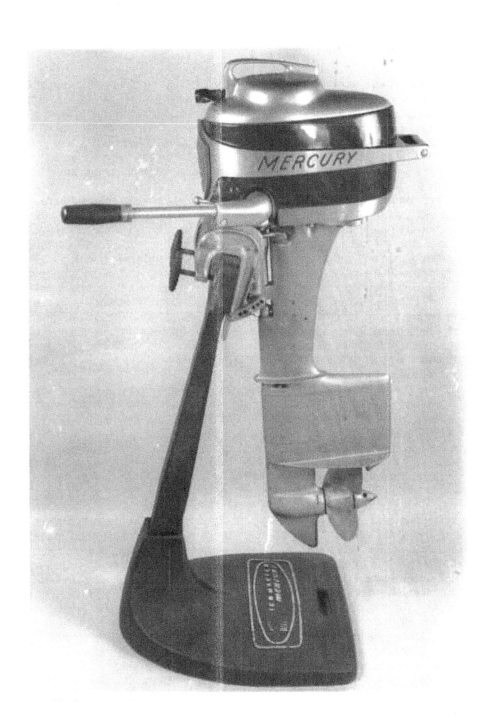

1928 Baby Whale Class "C" Racer

About 1925 the first outboard motors were produced that would propel a boat up and out of the water and on a firm planing attitude. From that point on outboarding grew at a phenomenal rate and outboard racing events were broadcast nationally along with major league sports. Marathon events were staged on almost any body of water that stretched for more than a few miles. The Around Manhattan Marathon and the Albany, NY to NYC Run were but a few yearly events staged in the East. Boat and motor manufacturers were fiercely competitive in their quest of the latest endurance or speed record with which to spearhead their advertising campaigns. The New York to Miami
Run was accomplished several times using equipment such as the Baby Whale pictured here.
Baby Whales were manufactured by D. N. Kelley & Son Inc of Fairhaven, MA. A brass plate on the bow stated "The Famous Whaling City Boats" - The World's Best Boats. Indeed they were quality built and reflected the latest design achievements of the period. Several outboard powered models were offered, starting with a 12 foot lapstrake tender and ending with a 16 foot mahogany runabout. Also produced were the step plane class racers, the term step plane denoting the two point hydro configuration at a time before the distinction between hydroplane and runabout became firmly implanted in outboard racing. These early racing boats had grab rails located where the steering wheels were positioned a few years later. The driver grasped this rail with one hand while steering and controlling the throttle of his outboard by reaching back to the elongated twist grip tiller handle with the other. The position was hardly comfortable, nor did it allow for good balance, but such hardships were gladly endured by those hardy souls joyously committed to this exciting new sport.
The Class "C" Baby Whale shown here was restored to mint condition by Bill Andrulitis of Manchester, MA who is a member of the Antique Outboard Motor Club. While Bill is readying a 30 cu. in. Class "C" Evinrude Speeditwin of the same vintage for use on his Whale, he is presently using a 20 inch Class "B" Lockwood Chief, also a popular racing engine of the day. Although Bill expects speeds in the high thirties from

the "C" engine the smaller Lockwood is performing in the thirty MPH range which compares favorably to the speed achieved when both boat and motor were new.
It is not really known how many vintage outboard hulls remain in existence.
Although produced in large numbers, they were and are highly disposable items, much more so than outboard motors of the same period. Though larger, more ruggedly constructed inboards were often times kept around because they contained engines which might someday be rejuvenated, outboard hulls with the passage of time and onslaught of the elements were apt to become simply a pile of rotten wood. On the other hand due to their smaller size and lighter weight they were more likely to have been stored inside, but therein lies another ailment common to some that survive today. Improper storage has left many of the fragile craft hopelessly warped and twisted. One might therefore think that these old hulls are a rare and valuable commodity, but such is not the. case. The reason is that demand is exceedingly low. Even a hull serving in good condition requires a certain amount of attention before it can be used and agreat deal of care to keep it in decent shape. Interest in old outboard hulls remains basically with some members of the Antique Outboard Motor Club which incidentally are few and far between. So if you find yourself in possession of one of these relics and would like to see it go to a good home where this comer of boating history is being preserved you might think about advertising it in the Antique Outboard Motor Club newsletter. The address is A.O.M.C.I. Newsletter, 326 W South St, Oconomowoc, WI 53066. The price for the ad is $2.00 and if one would like a copy of the newsletter in which the ad appears a SASE and 10 Cents should be included.

SPECIFICATIONS

Type Class Length Beam
Construction

Step Plane "C"
14 .
46"
Mahogany Plank over Spruce Ribs & Stringers. Canvas Deck

1917 Caille 5 Speed

The name Caille, while holding no particular significance to the younger generation, nevertheless remains well recognizable as a major manufacturer of outboard motors to most of us, middle aged and older who had anything at all to do with small powered boats way back when. Caille (which rhymes with "pail", so the advertising said) ceased outboard production in 1935, however the company was already an established maker of small inboard engines when in 1913 they produced their first outboard; a 2 horsepower rudder controlled, battery ignition single.

During the two decades that followed Caille earned a reputation for building well designed, quality engines. They also became known as an industry innovator early on in their existence and a couple of their special features are well worth noting in this 1917 model.

Caille was the first to introduce the auto rewind starter to the outboard in 1915. Although the unit worked well under normal usage, its fragile mechanism could give problems if an operator became upset with a balky, hard starting motor. The starting cord however, which was a cured horsehide strap was almost indestructible and this particular engine still retains its original in perfect condition.

Another Caille first was their variable pitch propeller as applied to the outboard which the company referred to as the "5-speed" on motors so equipped. The mechanism was released with the press of a button on the end of the tiller handle. The tiller was then raised or lowered to five separate locked positions which adjusted the propeller blades to two speeds reverse, one neutral, or two forward. The feature proved rugged and dependable and with the absence of distinct gear changes the outboard could be "shifted" from full speed forward to full speed reverse while going at top speed. In later years this unit became known as the Caille Multiflex and could be ordered on the entire line of outboards. Even by today's standards the versatility of a 15 or 21 HP electric starting Caille Multiflex would be hard to surpass.

[1]

The engine pictured here was restored by Dave Batchelder of Billerica, MA. This superb piece of work by Dave even included an exact reproduction of the original decal. During the company's existence, Caille produced many thousands of outboards and not surprisingly a great many are still in existence today, although the majority of these still in use are in the hands of members of The Antique Outboard Motor Club.

The Caille brothers Adolph and Arthur did not restrict their production to outboards. They also produced slot machines. However another item that may be recognized by the greatest number of people around today, although itself not having been manufactured in many years, is the huge penny weight scale. Remember that tall black pedestal with the big white dial on which was printed "Your weight for one cent"? A once common sight in drug stores or on the sidewalks outside, these familiar figures have also all but disappeared.

SPECIFICATIONS

HP	2 @ 700 RPM
Bore & Stroke	2.62" x 2.50"
Weight	60 lbs.
Price	$100

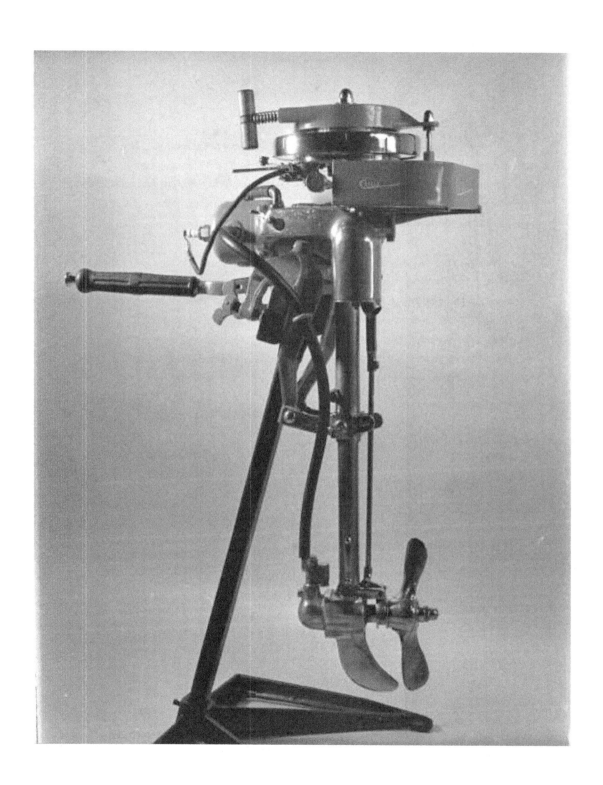

1958 16-1/2 Lyman & 1958 Evinrude Lark 35 HP

Perhaps no other period in small boat history has offered the variety of products to the boating public as did the mid to late 1950s. Wood, that traditional material of the industry, was waging its last battle to retain its place of dominance only to fade almost completely from the scene during the sixties. Aluminum had gained increasing popularity after World War II and during these years many companies jumped on the "Lightness-no upkeep" bandwagon. The third and most significant material to emerge during this period was of course, fiberglass. You could do almost anything with fiberglass and designers often did in these days of no holds barred creativity. Everything, it seemed, was supposed to look like a jet plane or a rocket ship. One only has to look at the years 1957 through 1959 to see how far the auto industry went. Some of these cars didn't look like they would stay on the ground and with three or four hundred horsepower, some didn't. Unlike the ho-hum attitude of today, styling was a big thing in the fifties. The new models were eagerly awaited and hardly a single mass produced product survived untouched. Many innovations and trends started in the 50s. Some lasted only a few years while others are still with us. Tail fins disappeared in the mid sixties as did the automotive horsepower race. The outboard horsepower race, however is still going strong.

The point of this nostalgia is naturally its relationship to their peak in design and quality. A molded plywood runabout of hat period for example, was a lightweight, durable, and virtually leakproof hull although they still required the usual upkeep associated with wood. Many people would not give up the look and feel of varnished mahogany and the wooden boat held its own from a sales standpoint. Wood, however by its very nature did not lend itself well to some of the futuristic designs of the day, though some manufacturers joyously tacked tail fins on existing models, more often than not resulting in some ugly caricature. AristoCraft, by comparison built a plywood boat totally around styling themes of the day and carried the effort off quite well. Many makers of wood hulls, however, chose to remain strictly traditional in their approach and a loyal segment of the boat buying public responded by purchasing large numbers of these hulls. Lyman Boat Works of Sandusky, Ohio was one of the most popular of these manufacturers and built a complete line of boats from small outboards to inboards well above the twenty foot range, all using the same time honored, clinker-built design. The 16-1/2 model shown here showed up at the Eighth Annual Antique and Classic Boat Show at Weirs Beach, New Hampshire as hosted by The New England Chapter of the Antique and Classic Boat Society. The Lyman and the 1958 Evinrude 35 HP Lark which were originally purchased together are owned by Paul and Sandra Lewis of Rochester, NH and are in absolute mint original condition. The rig will do 30 MPH with one person aboard and will readily plane 4 adults. It has no trouble pulling a water skier at a comfortable, if not hair raising, clip and will even pull two if those skiing will give the engine a little help with deep water starts. The Evinrude Lark, incidentally, sported newly designed shrouds for 1958 in keeping with the then current styling trends. Not quite as wild looking as some, Evinrude chose to appear at home on a Lyman as well as the all out futuristic fiberglass jobs. This was the third year for the Lark model which in '56 and '57 was Evinrude's top of the line ultimate outboard. In 1958 however, the Lark had to take second billing to the 50 HP V-4 Starflight, which along with the Johnson V-4, were the industry's first 4 cylinder V-engined outboards and the forerunners of all OMC Vee-block motors of today.

Wood boats of the 1950s seem to be gaining a limited popularity among antique and classic boat buffs usually associated with inboards and frequently one will turn up at boat shows of this nature. However, for anyone considering the purchase and restoration of one of these hulls beware of inflated prices some dealers in old boats are trying to get for these craft. Although, boats of the quality of this Lyman and others like it are admittedly in a class by themselves within this category, in this man's opinion there are many more people out there selling these boats in order to get into the newer, no maintenance hull than there are people wanting to accept the upkeep of these old boats. Those wanting them for show purposes are few and far between. Boats of the 1950s are still not all that ancient and there are a great many to be found on and off the water.

Specifications

1958 Evinrude Lark

Type	alternate firing twin
Bore & Stroke	3-1/16" x 2-3/4"
Cubic Inches	40.5
Horsepower	35 @ 4500 RPM
Electric Starting	Standard
Weight	138 lbs
Price	$635.00

1958 Lyman

Length	16-1/2'
Construction	Clinker-built
Options	Windshield & Canvas Top
Price	from $680.00

L. Carpenter

Antique Corner
1937 Evinrude Sportfour

By the mid thirties the outboard motor was well on the road to becoming a fairly civilized piece of equipment. True, there was still a company or two that continued to market the pow - boom - bang, bare bones variety of engine; the type that might eat your hand or grab your tie if you weren't careful and sounded like a box of golf balls crashing down a flight of stairs. But for the most part the industry seemed headed toward a product that promised convenience, dependability, safety, and yes, even style.

Outboard advertisements of the teens and early twenties had frequently pictured a silken clad lass lovingly caressing a crank start "rowboat motor" and proclaiming with a soft smile that she dearly loved this quaint little device that without a moments hesitation would whisk her across the lake to that afternoons lawn party. The truth was of course that had she somehow managed to start the thing it would most certainly have scared her half to death and quite likely broken one or more of her delicate bones in the process. After all, the term "knucklebuster", though firmly denied by all ad-men so engaged, was widely circulated by the outboard buying public. However, I really don't intend to cast these early outboards aside with such a derogatory remark. In their own way they were marvelous machines and performed remarkably well within their limitations. But with long hair, fragrant perfume, and polished nails? Give me a break! So much for the truth in advertising of the day.

As time went on the product began to catch up with the claims of its manufacturers. Lethal hand crank knobs which became invisible whirling clubs atop revolving flywheels were finally removed or at least recessed to release the operator from the shock of suddenly disappearing appendages. Spark plugs were at last hidden beneath their own caps or covers thereby depriving an owner from the joy of receiving his very own electrical charge along with his motor.

From a standpoint of convenience and further safety a beginning was made to clean up the whole outer surface of the outboard so that when carrying the engine an individual would be less likely to find a carburetor or other uncomfortable component probing at his navel. However, the outboard motor was not becoming tame; it was simply aquiring manners.

In 1934 Evinrude was celebrating its silver aniversary and consequently made a big splash with its most advanced and extensive line of outboards to date. They ranged from the Sport Single rated at 2.2 H.P. all the way to the fire breathing four cylinder, 60 cubic inch model "460" racing engine rated at 54.2 H.P. Between these extremes resided eleven other basic models. Some of these motors were offered with electric starting including the 8.5 H.P. Fleetwin. Also featured was an all electric outboard which curiously enough was driven soley by the electric start unit of the aforementioned models. Other features of the line included a flash start primer, carburetor silencer, ball and roller bearings, rubber mounted powerheads, simplified controls and more. Prices went from $69.95 to $495.00 which simply proves that the outboard has never been inexpensive.

The big news of 1934, however, was something called "Hooded Power". The original ad copy really said it best. ----"Forget your first temptation to see whats under the hood. Forget cylinders and carburetor and every engine part. They're all there, snugly protected under the gleaming streamlined cowlings. Chances are, unless you're curious, you'll never see what they look like throughout a seasons use.". It kind of takes your breath away doesn't it? Ad men, it seems, never change, but actually here they were not far from the truth.

Over the next couple of years "Hooded Power" spread further through the line and the 1937 Sportfour pictured here illustrates the visual effects of the feature very well. The Sportfour was rated as a medium sized motor and was right in the middle of no fewer than five four cylinder opposed models that

Evinrude built over a period of two decades ending in 1950. The smallest was just over five horsepower; the largest was fifty. Incidently, Evinrude did not reintroduce the four cylinder outboard until 1958, this time in the more modern alternate firing configuration which of course is still very much alive. The old Sportfour, however, was and is no slouch for smoothness, its finely balanced powerplant having the firing impulses of an alternate firing twin.

Actually many outboards of the thirties can still be used and enjoyed as contemporary engines because in many ways they are not all that far removed from todays motors. I would include the Sportfour in this catagory. Although not quite as forgiving as current models in the starting and fuel mixture departments, the engine operates well once one is familiar with the controls. The long tiller handle incorporates a twist grip throttle, but for smooth running throughout the full R.P.M. range this must be manually syncronized with the separate spark advance under the flywheel. A little more getting used to, but nothing complicated. Finally, the Sportfour is a direct drive, foward speed engine only. There is no neutral or reverse. In the nineteen thirties that usually meant full speed ahead.

This particular engine was located a few years ago along with a half dozen other outboards of similar vintage residing peacefully in a boathouse attic where they had remained undisturbed for twenty years or more. The owners principal concern was to remove the motors from the space they occupied thereby allowing him to store more current items. The outboards were purchased for little more than scrap price. The Sportfour appeared to be in quite decent shape and received first attention. After a partial disassembly it was found that the only parts that required work was a clogged fuel line and both sets of ignition points. The Sportfour has a cast aluminum water pump impeller so cooling is not ever likely to be a problem as long as all water passages are clear. The cosmetic restoration that the old Evinrude has recieved to date can only be termed as "once over lightly". A complete cleaning, a little polish and a like amount of dull aluminum paint comprises the work done for the time being. Although the engine hasn't been used extensively since it was resurrected it is seen as a working motor to be enjoyed whenever the occasion arises. Possibly someday it will get the total restoration it deserves, new tank decals, etc.; but in the meantime it provides all the thrills anyone could ask for on the back of a twelve foot aluminum boat.

Specifications

No. of cylinders	4
Bore & Stroke	2" X 2"
Cubic Inches	25
Horsepower	16.2 @ 4000 R.P.M.
Weight	90 lbs.
Cost	$295.00
Rope Starting Model	

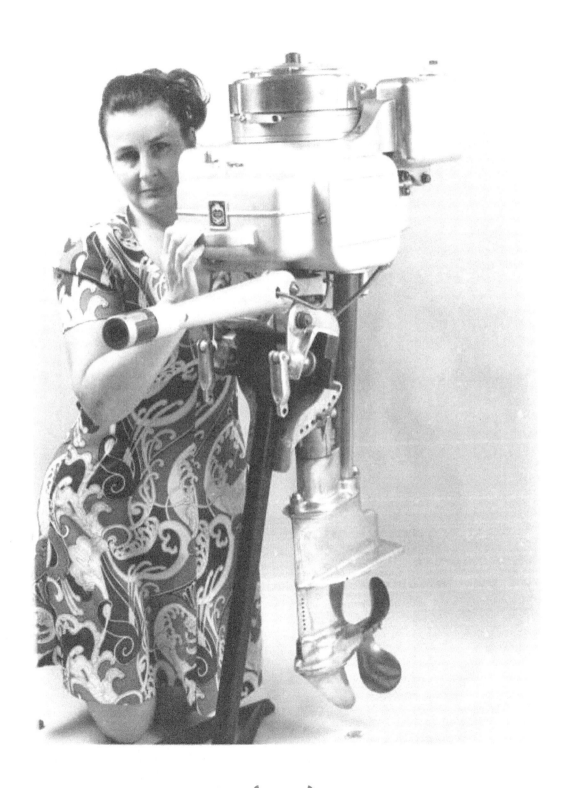

1954 Martin "200" Silver Streak

Again and again the stocky young man yanked the starter cord to its full exposed length with the powerful strokes of both arms as he stood precariously in the stern of the small plywood runabout that hot and humid August noon in 1955. Between breaths he cursed the engine, its manufacturer and anything else he could think of. The outboard jumped and twisted helplessly under this onslaught, sometimes lifting its lower unit out of water; but aways keeping its mechanical mouth shut as if silently mocking its attacker. It's never going to start for that fool, I thought.

A girl, slightly younger, but of equally overweight proportions sat in the small forward cockpit of the boat, her arms outstretched grasping gunwhales to steady herself against the rocking motion her older brother was producing with his almost frantic efforts to start the engine. Her expression was one of complete and utter boredom inching towards frustration.

"That guy is really going berserk," commented Kenny Anderson as he sat on the dock his feet lightly steadying the bow of my small aluminum runabout.

"Yeah," I said absently, not taking my eyes from that ugly little boat as it bobbed in the water perhaps a hundred fifty yards up the lake and a similar distance from shore. I knelt in the stern of my boat and glanced at my own outboard, a gleaming new 10 HP Martin "100", a dealer leftover long standing but scarcely three weeks old as far as I was concerned. A new ".22" rifle, a bicycle, or perhaps even an outboard motor can sometimes claim a special place in the heart of a 15 year old boy. Though simply an object to be used to serve some common purpose an item such as this can achieve the status of a silent friend to be talked to, cared for, and never be forgotten. I grasped the tiller handle of the motor and looked again to the lake where the spectacle was still going on.

"That will never happen to you," I said softly and gripped the handle a little tighter

The outboard being so soundly thrashed by the bully was the top-of-the-line big brother to my own. An almost mystical engine of supreme reputation, it was the only Martin "200" I had ever seen.

At last the bully ceased his efforts to start the motor and breathlessly turned to yell at his sister who reached to the bottom of the boat and thrust the short paddle back over her shoulder without turning her head or even shifting her gaze. Her brother, paddle in hand, looked around to orientate himself then took a few quick dips directing the boat towards shore. At this point the sister finally turned and unleashed a series of unintelligible remarks at the bully. After replying in kind he once again looked at the outboard.

"What?" Kenny yelled to no one in particular and involuntarily tried to stand on the forward deck of my boat, his expression was one of disbelief. The guy on the lake was actually beating the outboard with his paddle. I could see a monstrous dent in the side of the gas tank as part of the paddle splintered away. "The guy is going berserk," Kenny repeated, then added "he's insane!"

"Stop! Cut it out, you idiot!" I screamed at the top of my lungs. "Lets get out there" I said turning to Kenny. "Untie the bow".

I started the "100" in neutral with a quick pull and reached for the stern line.

"Look! Look what he's doing." Kenny said as he tossed the bow line into the boat.

The bully's hands were at the transom clamps and a second or two later the motor rose into the air as he held it chest high. I yelled and screamed some more, exactly what, I don't remember, but probably a good share of it couldn't be printed here. The sister was of course still yelling at her brother now from a standing position and

2

from shore came the animated shouts of an older man I knew to be the father as he literally jumped up and down on the end of their wharf.

Whether from intent or fatigue or both the bully half dropped and half threw the outboard. The powerhead struck the transom a glancing blow just before the resounding splash covered the boat with water. The sudden movement of the departing outboard caused the sister to lose her balance and she tumbled backward toward the bow. The fore deck proved to be no match for her descending derriere and the sounds of disintegrating plywood could be plainly heard as she crashed through to the bottom of the boat. Only her head, arms and legs were visible and her yells quickly changed to cries of pain.

Another time I have no doubt we would have laughed ourselves silly, but I think we were both drained by what we had seen.

"You going to be around this afternoon?" I asked Ken. "I'm going to head on back home for a while, but I'll be back over later."

"Yeah, I guess so," Kenny said, taking a last look out on the lake before walking the length of the dock to his parent's summer camp, shaking his head and muttering to himself. "I'll see you after lunch," he turned to add.

I slipped the "100" into forward gear and pointed the Aero Craft toward home hardly noticing that the father had managed to get a rowboat almost out to where his lovely children were still making quite a racket.

My anger started to rise up again as the boat clipped smoothly along. I had tried to talk to the guy once, I thought, but had gotten nowhere. I had told him that he had the engine set up all wrong, tilted forward like that and the load was too much for the narrow planing area of his boat which was a mess anyway. He hadn't appreciated that and I had gotten the idea he and his father had built the thing and had somehow forgotten what they were making halfway through the project. On several occasions during the past month I had seen thew boat with brother and sister aboard, its bow pointed to the sky and the engine winding for all it was worth, going nowhere at a slow pace. Other times, I had seen the boat dead in the water with the occupants taking turns to start the motor. Only once had I actually seen the boat up on plane if you could call it that. The thing had skipped across the water in a violent porpoising action and I couldn't believe that the keel was slightly convex all the way to the transom like that of a sailboat. The plywood bottom extended past the transom to form after planes of some weird configuration that almost encircled the tower housing of the outboard in some kind of intended engine well. Of course it is a well known fact that teenagers have all the answers concerning whatever they might be engaged in at any given moment, but as I neared home there was one thing that I had become increasingly sure of. The Martin "200" had become fair game as soon as it hit the water and one way or another I was going to have that engine before nightfall.

During the 1930s George Martin became well known in outboarding circles as a designer, builder and successful racer of outboard motors. Among George's innovations was the installation of poppet valves to the intake system of the two cycle outboard engine, an idea which worked extremely well and produced a motor having superior idling qualities and an excellent horsepower per cubic inch ratio. George Martin's dream was to manufacture a complete line of his own outboards and shortly after World War II this dream became a reality. In 1946 as a division of National Pressure Cooker Company of Eau Claire, Wisconsin, Martin Motors produced its first outboards in the form of the Martin "60," an 11 cubic inch alternate firing twin rated at a very healthy 7.2 horsepower. The engine weighed only 37 lbs. In a few short years Martin fielded several models ranging from 2-1/3 HP to 10 HP and in just that space of time these high quality, superb performing outboards secured a growing number of very loyal buyers, the size of which was becoming a frequent if not popular topic of conversation at OMC and Mercury dealerships.

4

As time went on the only deficiency of the Martin line appeared to be the absence of an engine in the "big motor" category. Other companies were building 25 HP motors and Martin owners were crying for something larger than a ten. In the summer and fall of 1953 rumors of that something began to filter up to the New Hampshire Lakes Region and places where people talked outboards, excitement began to grow and no one was more excited than I.

"Its the Martin "200" and its called the Silver Streak!"

"The Silver Streak, huh. Really?"

"Its rated at 20 HP, but I'll tell you this. It's no ordinary 20 HP." This last was sometimes uttered in hushed tones capped with a knowing smile.

"Really?"

"I guess the guys at Mercury are real nervous. They're getting the idea they can kiss class "B" goodbye and I can tell you this, they don't like it one bit. I'll tell ya this "200" is the Ferrari of outboards!"

"Really? Oh boy!"

Understand that no one disliked Mercury but the Mercs had their own way for a long time and of course everyone loves an underdog. And a dark horse from Martin of all places. Hot Damn!

Next came stories of the preproduction exploits of the "200."

" Twin Martin Silver Streaks took everything in sight in the Mississippi River Marathon! Yeah everything! Even the Merc Mark 40s. I understand the "200" has a sound all its own. Kind of a high pitched metallic wail." All of this had been from the

Sporting Goods store proprietor down the lake who had had a somewhat limited dealer association with Martin.

"Really? Wow! How soon are they going to be shipping them? When are you going to get some?"

"I don't know exactly, but soon. Maybe any day now. I've got a standing order."

I didn't know it then, but that very day was probably the height of the Martin "200" excitement and it was all downhill from there. Even by Martin standards the local dealership was a small one, it being a secondary part of a sporting goods store and their long awaited Martin "200" never did arrive. From there, circumstances combined to sink the Silver Steak and as a result, the whole Martin line.

The "200" proved to be expensive to build partly as a result of production difficulties and a slim profit margin all but went out the window. Actual introduction was somewhat delayed and when sparse shipments finally got underway many people were tired of waiting. In the company's attempt to establish a reputation of speed through eventual entry into class "B" racing as well as with the hot rod boat enthusiast Martin made a serious error. They marketed the "200" with the nearly square gear ratio in favor of a more standard lower unit configuration that would have suited a far greater number of consumers. Indeed more than a few buyers did not fully realize what this really meant until they started the engine on the stern of their family runabout. Many more people were upset over the "200"'s lack of pulling power than were inspired by its breakneck speed capabilities when set up correctly on the right boat. These misunderstandings were greatly enhanced by a lack of communication between the factory, dealer and customer. Indeed what the pubic bought was very close to a pure racing engine with very little else needed to make it one. For instance, the factory conversion kit to make the "200" lower unit race ready was comprised of a shorter drive shaft, a pointed gear case cap to replace the rounded one and a shortened intermediate tower housing. It sold for $32.00. The gear ratio remained the same.

In a frantic effort to correct this one basic mistake Martin readied another "200" model referred to as the Silver Liner. This engine it was said had a full forward, neutral and reverse twist grip controlled lower unit which housed a more civilized gear ratio. Also the Silver Liner had calmed the Streak's somewhat finicky nature so the story went. However it was all in vain because by that time Martin had gone down for the third time. It is not known, at least by this writing if any Silver Liners actually made it to the market place.

Getting back briefly to that summer afternoon of 1955, my attempt to retrieve that unfortunate "200" from the bottom of the lake was extremely short-lived. A quick look at the chart of the lake revealed a depth in that area of just over a hundred feet with a mucky bottom. Having thought in terms of water half that deep, I was crestfallen. Scuba diving as a sport was still in its infancy during the mid fifties and I had planned on using a tiny 15 minute aqualung a friend of mine had bought from a mail order catalog. We had a great time chasing small mouth bass to a depth of 35 or 40 feet and I felt capable of stretching this to 60 if the prize was a Martin "200". But 100 feet? Even in my enthusiasm I knew it would be foolhardy and unfortunately I knew of no one else that would attempt it. In the hundreds of times I have since driven over that exact spot with other boats I must admit it was some years before I did not think of that Martin "200" and by the time I was capable of looking for it I confess the urgency of that August afternoon had somewhat faded coupled with the realization that by that time the engine was a worthless hunk of metal. I am quite certain that no one else attempted to get the motor so in all likelihood it is still down there in the muck.

Martin Motors stopped operations in 1955 and the outboard industry as a whole was the poorer for it. Although that occurred some 27 years ago more than a few Martins are still in regular service, a fact that attested to their quality and durability. As for the Silver Streak? Had the "200" been afforded a better chance for survival who knows what it might have accomplished.

POSTSCRIPT: Several years ago my wife expressed a desire to buy me a special present. She specified that it be something that I had always wanted, but for whatever reason had never been able to acquire. I didn't hesitate for a second. A Martin "200" and a Lockheed P-38 Lightning, I told her. The engine pictured here is a result of her efforts. It was built largely from NOS components. She is still working on the P-38.

Specifications

Powerhead	alternate firing twin
Bore & Stroke	2-1/2 x 2-1/32
Cubic Inches	19.94
Gear Ratio	15 to 16
Integral fuel tank capacity	10 pints
Auxiliary fuel tank	6 gallons
Weight	70 pounds
Cost	$399.75

Special features

Mechanically controlled poppet valves - 2 per cylinder. Inboard controlled tilt angle engine trim adjustable while engine is underway - all Martin models integral and auxiliary gasoline tank gauges. High speed gear ratio - (15-16)

L. Carpenter

A. C. Postscript

In the April, 1982 Antique Corner I related the story of the 1954 20 HP Martin "200" Silverstreak, the largest and the last model introduced by this manufacturer of fine outboard motors. The Silverstreak, as marketed, carried nearly a one to one lower unit gear ratio. This was fine for racing, but not ideally suited for general family use. For this reason and others the Martin 200 was not popular nor was it produced in great numbers and shortly thereafter the company ceased all outboard production.

Some time before the end finally came the company announced a new "200" model to be called the Silverliner. This outboard was to have Martins first full forward, neutral, and reverse gearshift and a more reasonable lower gear ratio plus a few other minor modifications.

At the time of this column the best information I could gather indicated that it was doubtful that any Silverliners were actually produced. Quite recently, however, I have heard from --- I believe the term is "informed sources", that at least one Silverliner was indeed produced and that it was acquired by a Martin employee when the company went out of business. A further rumor indicated that the engine may have been taken to Canada, but there the story ends.

The obvious question: Does this motor still exist? And if so, where is it? If indeed the Silverliner is alive and reasonably well, it would be a shame to lose even this small corner of outboard history, at this late date.

Dear Jean,

Jim Youngs suggested that I write a short postscript to be included at the end of a regular Antique Corner column concerning my search for information on the Amarc diesel outboard.

This I have done and in addition I have included a second such postscript which is self-explanatory.

I was wondering if these postscripts might do well as a semi-regular addition to the column. They could and probably would be independent from the column with which they appeared. They could be of the searching-for variety. They might update or refer back to a previous column as does this Martin postscript or they might take the form of a book review of some out-of-print publication the antique boat and motor enthusiasts could look for to compliment their interests.

What do you think?

Best regards,

Larry Carpenter

L.Carpenter

Antique Corner
Hand Driven Outboards

I'd rather do it myself, so the saying goes and certainly throughout this century a solid segment of the populace has evoked this sentiment to shun the efficient application of motive power in favor of muscle power to transport themselves from place to place. The introduction of the motorcycle way back when certainly did not spell the end of the bicycle and quite recently a group of enterprising souls went so far as to perfect a muscle-powered aircraft. The subject discussed here, however, relates to the hand powered outboard device and a brief history thereof.

The model on the left reflects the state of the art in its very early stages and dates from the late 1800s. Its basic construction is of wood and its mechanical components; chain sprocket, chain, etc. were taken from a bicycle. The two blade fan-type propeller is of undetermined origin. The unit is very well constructed, but appears to be a one-of-a-kind hand built item rather than a company manufactured one. The device must be screwed or bolted to the stern of the boat. The separate hinged rudder is controlled by a light sash cord type line which could be extended around the gunwales of the boat so steering could be accomplished from any location by someone other than the person providing the motive power. Reverse is obtained by simply cranking in the oposite direction. The unit is hinged on the transom enabling the operator to cruise over submerged objects or to raise it out of water when beaching the boat. Actually if one can picture a crude electric motor substituted for the horizontal crank rod the result would be a device very much like what is generally recognized to be the first outboard motor introduced by Gustave Trouve at the Paris Exposition in 1881.

The next model in line is the Ro-Peller made by Ra-Sco Mfg. Co. Shelbyville, Ind. in 1931. It operates much (the same) as the previous unit, but attains higher prop speeds through the use a large upper gear and driveshaft arrangement. The lower unit is designed along the lines of a modern outboard and steering is done in the conventional manner of changing thrust direction.

Beside the Ro-Peller resides a unit that appears nearly identical, but which incorporates a marked difference in its internal mechanism. Unfortunately when this particular example was located it was missing the rear cover to the upper crank housing and on this cast aluminum cover was almost certainly written the name of its manufacturer. However, an educated guess can be made as to its origin. Ro-Peller is said to have been in business little more than a year, so I would tend to assume this unit to have been built somewhat later by another company that purchased the Ro-Peller interests and used some of its components to market a hand crank outboard of their own. An attempt was made to reduce production costs and herein lies that marked difference between it and the Ro-Peller. Instead of a driveshaft and gear arrangement this model used a series of drive and guide pulleys and a continuous vee belt not unlike an automotive fan belt to transmit crank power to the cupped three bladed prop. Operation of this unit is not as smooth as the Ro-Puller, the problem being a certain amount of resistance offered by the pully and belt arrangement. One reason these and other hand driven models did not make a go of it in the 1930s can be found in fact that during this period the small gasoline outboard motor market was locked in fierce competition and prices were low. Indeed near the end of the decade a $\frac{1}{2}$ h.p. single cylinder outboard could be purchased for less than $30.00.

Next we come to what can be justly termed a contraption. Manufactured during the 1950s in Detroit, the Hydro-Fin was designed to duplicate the movements of the caudal fin of a fish. Back and forth action of the tiller produces a similar motion of the sheet metal "fin". Metal stops limit fin travel from side to side thus producing foward thrust. Efficiency of this unit is extreamly low when compared to the other prop driven models.

The last outboard to the far right is the Man-U-Troll built by Universal Projects Inc. of Jacksonville, Florida. Its internal gear arrangement provides forward prop thrust through both up and down movement of the tiller handle. Slower propeller speeds permit the use of the extra large prop. Reverse is accomplished by rotating the device 180 degrees. This particular unit is from the $1960's$, however, the Man-U-Troll is still being manufactured today and appeared in this magazine a short time ago.

Hand driven outboards appeal to but a small segment of the mini-outboard market. Electrics make up the lions share and there are really small gas outboards available. The hand drives, however, have their place as well as their advantages. They are, of course, light weight and easily portable and may be used on those many small bodies of water where engines of any kind are prohibited. Though not quite capable of the speed of a pair of oars, the hand drives can be operated with one hand, a feature fishermen applaud while casting along a quiet shore line or slowly trolling around a patch of lily pads. Also the fact that hand drives require the use of one arm can be appreciated by those who unfortunately have but one to use.

Hand driven outboards require little or no maintenance, do not need gas or batteries and are ready to go any time at all. And last but not least: hand driven outboards are fun.

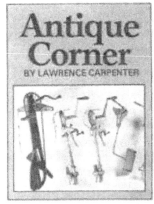

HAND-DRIVEN OUTBOARDS

1939 Clarke Troller

Scrapping all tradition! so stated the ad and in the late 1930s that is exactly what Clarke Engineering Co. of Detroit did in offering the public a revolutionary new outboard. Only 21 inches overall in length, weighs only 10-1/2 pounds, develops 1-2 HP, no pumps, no gears, no water jackets. Everything you ever wanted in an outboard and less. Sound good? Indeed it did, at least for a while.

Upon seeing a Clarke for the first time many people simply do not know what it is. When told it is an outboard motor they often reply, "you're kidding!" So let us take a closer look at this weird little bugger. The Clarke Troller is a submerged gasoline engine outboard, hence no water pump or water jackets are needed. Cooling water reacts directly on the cylinder wall. The prop shaft is simply an extension of the crankshaft, so any gearing is also unnecessary. Bolted directly atop the crankcase sits the lone vertical cylinder and behind it can be seen the curved cavitation plate which serves a second purpose that I'll touch upon later. The cavitation plate is part of a watertight cast cover on the back of the cylinder and under this cover can be found the tiny spark plug and a set of ignition points, which by the way are operated by way of a pushrod, cam operated off the crankshaft. Ahead of the cylinder can be noticed a tube which travels upward to the base of the transom clamp and then downward well below water level. This is the exhaust pipe. Above the cylinder rises the long intake manifold visually ending at the small bulbous gas tank. On top of the gas tank a cast aluminum cover protects both spark coil and carburetor. Exiting to either side at the rear of this cover are the operating controls. On the port side are the choke and throttle. Needle valve is to the starboard. Here also is found the gas cap and tank vent. The long cord protruding from the very top of the unit must be connected to a 6 volt battery, the only external piece of equipment needed to operate this battery ignition motor.

So there. If you think you have all this new outboard geography firmly implanted in your mind we can get on to the fun part, that is, running the engine. Starting a Clarke Troller can be quote an experience that first few times. It can even be dangerous. First of all, after being fastened securely to the transom by the single clamp the unit is raised to a horizontal position and the tilt lock pin on the upper part of the transom clamp body is inserted to hold the engine in place. After setting the throttle, choke and needle valve and making sure the gas vent is open, the starter cord is wound clockwise around the tiny rope sleeve on the propeller hub. Yes, that's what I said. In the picture you may notice the starter cord is hanging from the ring type skeg, a handy place to keep it when the Clarke Troller is not in use which in many cases is almost always. Incidentally, the propeller blades are razor sharp and must be individually set, a necessity not really designed to drive the operator crazy while it strives to achieve a balanced propeller, but rather to eliminate the required mechanism to synchronize the blades thereby presenting a more simple unit, a quality this whole outboard strives for. However, a very shallow pitch must be set and locked in place with provided set screws. It's really not that bad a procedure and once done the prop should not need to be touched thereafter. Now then, with one hand grasping the intake manifold to steady both yourself and the motor you may notice that with the starter cord wound tight your hand may be dangerously close to those prop blades and here we come to that other function of the cavitation plate. It serves as a guard between your hand and the prop. Quickly surveying this particular procedure one may easily conclude that a modern day OSHA official might have apoplexy at the mere sight of a Clarke Troller and obviously under current federal regulation the Troller would not be permitted to exist at all as Big Brother strives to take us all back to the safety of the womb. Hell, look what they've done to our lawnmowers. Well, enough of that, go ahead and pull the damn cord.

If the engine fails to start first pull and don't be surprised if it doesn't, you may be amazed at the super healthy compression of this tiny engine until you realize the limited mechanical advantage of that small diameter prop hub you're pulling on. Okay, let us assume that the engine has started and after getting over the racket it makes not unlike that of three or four model airplane engines, you have adjusted the controls so you are reasonably sure it will keep on running. Now you must get the powerhead into the water before it overheats. Incidentally, the official Clarke operating manual relates none of this. Do not simply pull the tilt locking pin and let the motor fall. The results may be catastrophic, resulting in damage to the transom, the motor, or both, to say nothing of your jangled nerves. While supporting the motor by grasping the intake manifold as before, release the locking pin and gently lower the motor into the water. Remember that once the prop bites into the water it's going to pull hard for the transom. Try to soften this blow as much as possible. If the engine hasn't stalled from the sudden load and further, passes the "Clarke ten-second test", that period during which many Trollers will simply stop for no readily apparent reason, you are off and running and able to relax, enjoy the scenery and try to stop shaking.

Be it known that I will not apologize for making light of the Troller. While I myself may not feel this way, many others long since gone have regarded this motor as a horrid little creature, an abomination if you will and I feel someone must speak for them, if only this once. However there was and is a group that regard Clarke Trollers, at least some Trollers as marvelous machines and while I have specimens that fall into both categories I must count myself as one of these. When acquired, it appeared to be in very good condition, but in need of some minor attention. The entire engine was covered with a thick layer of bright red paint some genius had applied with a half dozen swipes of a broom, so this was removed as all outer surfaces of this Clarke are cast aluminum and were not originally painted. The only mechanical work that the engine required was turning out a new needle valve. The original was damaged beyond repair. This accomplished, the motor started and ran quite well although it frequently would lapse into a four cycle mode; in other words it fired on every other revolution, a condition that was finally traced to the tiny spark plug being set at .025 instead of the mandatory .015 once an owners manual was secured. It is really amazing the power the Clarke Troller has for its size. It will push almost anything of reasonably light weight up to a length of 15 or 16 feet with quite satisfactory speed. Once in the water the fast turning little motor is very quiet and is so unobtrusive as to leave one to almost forget it is there. One further fact on this particular Clarke Troller. If you note directly underneath the gas tank you will see a separate section at the upper part of the manifold. This casting is added if one needs a little more length to the unit. Exhaust

3

pipes on the lengthier Clarke are also, of course, the same 3 inches longer. This model is therefore jokingly referred to as the long shaft model.

One spring a few years ago after following a lead on an old outboard I found myself at the door of a small older residence on the shore of a lake some miles to the west. A small wiry man in his late sixties appeared after my brief knock and upon introducing myself, I told him that I had heard that he had a particular engine and if so might it be for sale and could I take a look at it. The gentleman had a rustic air about him that matched his surroundings and displayed a willingness to talk seldom exhibited by other elderly Yankees who live alone in these parts. Yes, he still had the motor, but he hadn't used it in years and wasn't it a beautiful day.

"Come on in and let take a look at it. Its down cellar" he added. At the top of the stairs the old man turned and warned "watch your head here and be careful when we get down there. I've a bit of a problem this spring."

There was indeed a problem. There was 6 inches of water over the cellar floor.

"Watch your step" he said as the old man started off over a series on planks resting on concrete blocks. "The outboards over in that corner - I think".

There lying on the floor was most of a four cylinder, four cycle Fageol outboard. I immediately wrote the engine off in my mind as the old man stared down at the remains.

"I guess it's probably not much good now" he said.

I agreed that with the water being in the block for some time, the engine had, for all practical purposes, seen it's last days. I began to think about leaving.

Suddenly the man looked up and wagged a finger at me. "You know I had an old motor you'd probably be interested in seeing. You ever hear of a Clarke Troller?"

4

"Really?" I answered and gave him my full attention. Clarkes were not all that common. I replied that I knew what a Clarke Troller was and that I had a couple of them.

"Best damn fishing motor every built by man or beast", he went on. "Used it in salt water, lakes, ponds, you name it. The thing never gave me a bit of trouble."

This sounded a little odd to me. "What ever happened to it," I asked.

The old man gave me kind of a funny look, then once more shifted his gaze back to the unfortunate Fageol down in the water. "My son", he said softly and paused for several seconds. "We had what you would call a falling-out here a few years back. You know how it is," he said, but didn't look in my direction. "I haven't seen him since" he finally concluded in a very subdued tone.

For a minute there I thought the old gent might start to cry and I turned away momentarily to study the wall while I tried to think of something to say. It is not often pleasant to watch family skeletons come tumbling out of someone's closet.

"Yeah", snapped the old man suddenly as he fixed me with a stare. He looked angry. "Yeah, when he left he took my Troller with him and I haven't seen it since!"

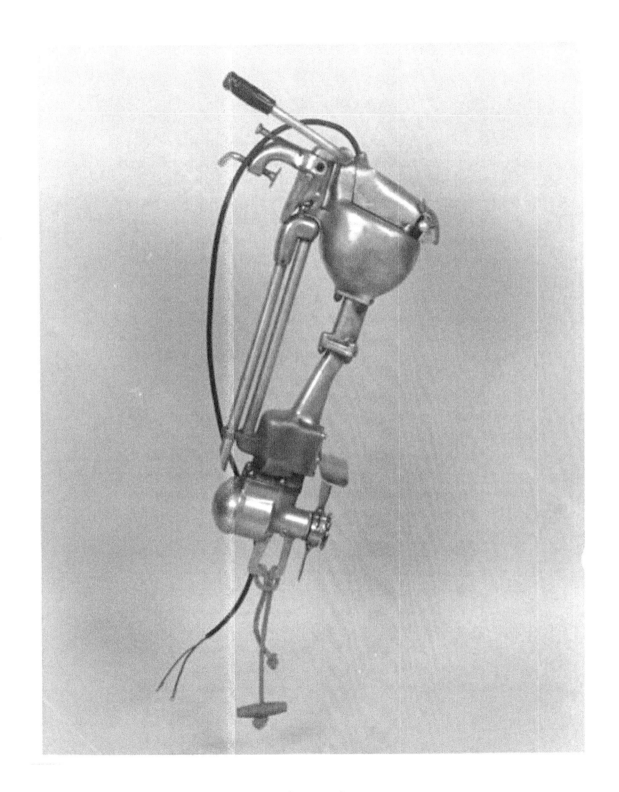

The Lockwood 72-TS

Shortly after World War I industry began to take a second look at aluminum. One dubious benefit of war-time production has always been the hurry-up, can't wait attitude of the military in a constant effort to throw superior hardware against the enemy. As a result, technology in general gets a shot in the arm and during the first World War much of the effort was centered around the use of various metals and their alloys. The marine industry of the day took special note of these goings on and in the early twenties aluminum began showing up in places where iron and bronze had been a tradition.

Outboard manufacturers had a special interest in aluminum. They had, after all, started an industry on the premise that they offered portable marine power plants and if the more widespread use of aluminum could make something lighter, it would naturally be more portable, hence afford greater appeal followed quickly by more sales. Not that aluminum was new. These companies had always used it, but had used it sparingly. Exhaust manifolds, for instance, had been cast from the light metal from the beginning, however an exhaust manifold required no particular strength, although aluminum did tend to dissipate heat quite well. Also aluminum took quite nicely to casting the company logo into the metal and the exhaust manifold became a popular location used by several early makers. But in those days the basic rule said that iron and steel would be used for strength and brass or bronze could be counted on to eliminate rust and corrosion. Besides, early aluminum was very expensive.

The early twenties saw a change. Better design and more advanced engineering tried to remove itself from a time when many parts were over-built as common practice. More importantly, aluminum had come of age. Metallurgical techniques of the day had improved the product greatly and carburetors, flywheels, transom clamps, lower units, and crankcases began showing up made from aluminum. Other parts were slower in coming as internal engine components like pistons and connecting rods, still had a while to wait and the first iron lined aluminum cylinders were almost a decade away. Nonetheless, manufacturers were happy with the results they achieved in such a short space of time. A two horsepower outboard motor instead of weighing seventy-five pounds or more now weighed less than half that amount, this not totally due the use of more aluminum, but certainly aluminum had proved invaluable toward this end.

However, as in all endeavors, enthusiasm often oversteps its bounds, at least a little bit, and this situation really created a backward step by the industry, requiring a second long look at a problem that persists to this day. The Lockwood outboard shown here along with some models of other makers illustrates the solution to the problem, a solution that found its roots in the tradition of a few years before. Pure aluminum simply would not stand up in the face of constant salt water use. Makers stressed that engines so used required special care that of course included flushing, rinsing, washing and oiling of the cooling system and outer surfaces of the motor, especially the lower unit, tower housing, etc. But to the majority of owners whose outboards might be in and out of the ocean on a daily basis, these tasks became sheer drudgery and were quickly neglected. The result naturally was a lower unit that corroded at an incredible rate. The answer to the problem was simple even though a bit regressive; return to using bronze on engines that were to see a great deal of ocean service. Happily, more corrosion resistant aluminum alloys would soon be on the scene and these "salt water models" would be deemed unnecessary.

The model designation 72-TS of this Lockwood breaks down as follows. The number 72 is the last two digits of the model year reversed; hence 1927. The letter "T" relates to the base model and the "S" signifies salt water use. Everything from the powerhead down excepting the transom clamp, but including the tilt adjustment slides is bronze. These parts on the standard model are aluminum.

The end result is an outboard of very striking appearance. Cylinders, muffler can, gas line and all water tubes are nickel plated. Flywheel and gas tank are polished aluminum and the polished bronze is as mentioned. The only painted surface is the aluminum handle grip which is black.

The Lockwood twin was one of the first handful of outboards that would propel a boat out of the water and on a firm planing attitude and so was in the midst of outboard racing when it started. The standard model in racing trim which merely dictated the removal of the exhaust system and carburetor intake tube, once established a world speed record of just under 25 MPH which stood for a short time.

This particular engine was in sad shape when it was located. It had remained outdoors for many years and was an object of interest to a group of children who had managed to remove and lose one of the cylinders which actually mattered little because the other was corroded into the water jacket and of no use anyway. The aluminum parts were badly pitted, someone had seen fit to beat on the lower unit with a hammer and an unknown variety of insects had built an elaborate nest in the magneto. However, once more in presentable condition, the Lockwood serves to illustrate outboarding at its best as it existed over fifty years ago.

Specifications

Type	opposed twin cylinder
Bore & Stroke	2-1/4" x 2"
Cubic inches	15.9
Horsepower	4+
Cost Standard Model	$145.00
Salt Water Model	$150.00

3

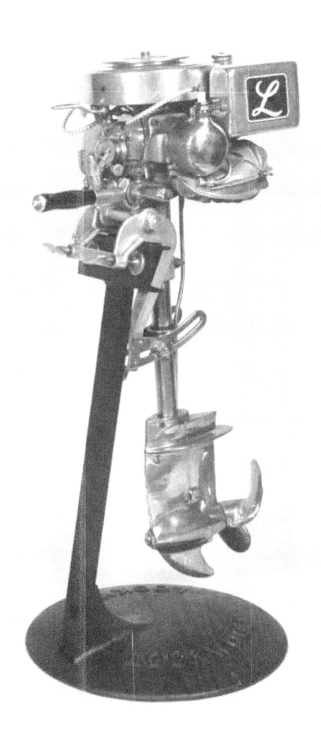

The Formation of OMC

In March of 1929 three of the five largest outboard motor companies of the day were brought together into one giant entity, Outboard Motors Corporation. This merger was the brainchild of Stephen F. Briggs of Briggs and Stratton, manufacturers of industrial engines. In the beginning Briggs sought to enhance the internal structure and marketing capabilities of his own firm, but soon became obsessed with the building of this huge outboard complex for its own sake. Evinrude Motors was the first company to be purchased. Evinrude had fallen on hard times during the early to mid twenties and had seen a quick succession of owners. The basic problem was that Evinrude had remained more or less motionless through this period of blossoming outboard technology while the competition had forged ahead with new designs. Beginning in 1927 Evinrude sought to correct this disadvantage with its new lineup of modern engines and two years later was well back in tune with the rest of the industry, however a deal was struck and Evinrude became the cornerstone of OMC.

Elto was not on the list of Stephen Briggs. Ole and Bess Evinrude had started the Elto company in 1921 when the powers to be at Evinrude had shown little or no interest in Ole's new light-twin outboard design. By 1929 Elto was a leader in the industry, having the year before introduced the Elto Quad, the first production four cylinder outboard. This new big powerful outboard had taken the boating public by storm and from a financial standpoint Elto was in an excellent position to continue as they were. For the Evinrudes, other factors of the pending deal held interesting possibilities. As a result of the merger, Ole would head the entire corporation and in doing so could exercise considerable control over his former namesake instead of competing against it. It was finally, for these considerations, that the Evinrudes said yes and Elto became the second piece of the puzzle.

Lockwood Motors had planted its outboard roots way back in 1913 when the industry was barely getting its collective props wet. Over the years the company had proceeded on a solid footing of honest value and quality. In the late twenties Lockwood

[1]

added to this foundation, design innovation and most of all, performance. Though not of the size of Evinrude or Elto, Lockwood Motors made a fine addition to the picture and indeed, completed it. Outboard Motors Corporation was off and running.

This was big news to say the least and the boating public wondered what might be in store for them. Each of the three brand names had loyal followings and many outboard enthusiasts feared that their favorite model might be swallowed up in some vast labyrinth of business expediency. OMC knew this and reacted to quell these and other fears by quickly laying their corporate cards on the table. A blitz of full page advertisements appeared in boating and sporting magazines. These ads stressed the continuance of individual model lines in their familiar company dress. Also touted were new features just around the corner such as electric starting, which made its appearance on the 1930 models. Other multipage advertisements didn't include a single picture of the outboard motor, but sought to explain and classify the image of Outboard Motors Corporation. One particular piece included the whole story in a nutshell and reads as follows - "The Elto Outboard Motor Company, the Evinrude Motor Company, and the Lockwood Motor Company are now merged into a single enterprise, Outboard Motors Corporation.

Ole Evinrude, builder of the first successful outboard, founder of the Evinrude Motor Company and the Elto Outboard Motor Company, became President and acting head of the Outboard Motors Corporation. The Lockwood, Elto, and Evinrude Companies each will maintain its personnel and identity as a manufacturing and merchandising Division of the Outboard Motors Corporation.

The products of the three Divisions will continue to be made and sold under the names they have always carried. Each Division will have its own dealer organization as formerly. Active, healthy competition will be continued - *But the Corporations entire resources of engineering and administrative strength and broadened manufacturing facilities will be unreservedly devoted toward increasing the quality and performance and value of each single product of each Division.*

2

The savings and economics of immense production will be given to buyers in motor values not heretofore possible.

The efforts of three outstanding successful engineering staffs, now merged and pointed toward mutual objectives, promise new expansions of outboard motor usefulness that will surpass and overshadow the notable developments of recent years.

The Outboard Motors Corporation automatically steps into a conspicuous leadership. In every racing class its products are officially the champions. The Lockwood "Ace" and Lockwood "Chief" were 1928 champions in classes A and B. The Evinrude "Speeditwin" has long held top place in class C. The Elto Quad holds not only the championship in classes D and E, but also America's fastest time trial and competition records. This racing supremacy, important though it is in the realm of sport, expresses its true value in terms of plain utility.

From these critical tests of materials, innovations and new engineering principles, has flowed steady inspiration for the building of service motors that are correspondingly superior in every phase of satisfactory day-in and day-out performance. Every motor in the broad range of models offered by Divisions of the Outboard Motors Corporation bears ample testimony to this fact.

The future looked bright and everything went fine: fine, that is up until the fall of 1929 when the stock market crash and resulting panic brought the entire business community to its knees and America as a whole began its long and weary trek through the "Great Depression". Somehow OMC managed to survive, but not without sacrifice, notably the dropping of the Lockwood Division from the masthead. Particularly sad was this loss because Lockwood was on the verge of introducing what is called "The Flying Four", a new four cylinder outboard in both C and D classes.

The picture continued to look bleak through 1930, 31 and most of 1932, however in 1933 business improved and by 1934 OMC was in surprisingly good shape once again, but not without one final tragic blow. During a fourteen month period ending on July 12, 1934 first Bess and then Ole Evinrude passed away. In not only the outboard industry, but American industry as a whole, has there been a finer more talented husband and wife team.

It was largely due to the Evinrudes that OMC survived and rebounded as quickly as it did. Many other manufacturers did not make it at all. However another industry leader before the crash of "29" still found itself barely able to keep its head above water in 1935 when OMC was nearly back to a "business as usual" stance. This company was Johnson Motors. Enter Stephen Briggs, chairman of the board of OMC and Ralph Evinrude, only son of Ole and Bess and President of OMC. In November of 1935 a controlling interest of Johnson Motors was purchased.

OMC now Outboard Marine Corporation, as we all know is still very much alive, its position as industry leader secure at least for the time being. There have, of course, been adjustments over the years as there will be in the future. Currently concern may well be focused on the increasing number of foreign imports on American waters, but hopefully lessons learned by the domestic auto industry will not be lost on the outboard community. Surely the end result will be worth the effort.

ANTIQUE CORNER

by

Lawrence Carpenter

GRAND CRAFT 24 FOOTER

1930 was a strange year. It was also a tragic year for many Americans who were to find hard times following at their heels well into the middle of the decade. The stock market crash in the fall of 1929 had badly shaken the economic structure of the country right down to its foundation; however at the outset not everyone percieved these goings on in the same manner. An individual whose fortune was deep rooted in the market, but perhaps whose family had drifted away from hands-on business involvement over the last couple of generations may well have viewed the sidewalk as a final destination as he looked out the tenth floor window of his New York hotel suite. Faced with losing everything, a great many others followed this path of escape. However, right next door to that now deceased gentleman on the tenth floor may well have resided a representative of another faction; a man on a business trip whose company now lay in shambles, quietly contemplating what to do next. He may well have believed that this sudden economic collapse was but a temporary state and that the economy would right itself almost as quickly if everyone kept their head. Many held this viewpoint and attempted to plunge ahead on a business-as-usual footing. More likely though, he realized that to survive the months and years ahead, his company would have to scratch and claw for any reason to exist at all and that he must fight to his last breath to keep it alive. It is largely through the efforts of men such as these that the country made it through the great depression intact and indeed if it had been allowed to slip much further our whole social structure may well have evolved very differently.

The boating industry as a whole was made up of people such as these. It was basically a young industry so the majority of those who had started it all were still in control and they knew what it would take to stay afloat. Many companies failed, to be sure, but many more survived to reach the calmer waters of the late 1930's. If one were to pick up, say the January 1930 Show Issue of Motor Boating, it would be hard indeed to conclude that these were anything other than the greatest of times. Pleasure boat manufacturers and related marine supplies put their best face forward in this one-inch-thick magazine and is full of multi-page advertisements elaborately done to resemble company catalogs. At the forefront of these are the ads for inboard mahogany runabouts. Names such as Dodge, Hackercraft, Sea Lyon, DeeWite, Dart, Aco, and ChrisCraft gave firm notice that such boats were here to stay.

Although having been in business a scant eight years, ChrisCraft was billed as the worlds largest manufacturer of mahogany motor boats ranging from a 20' runabout to a luxurious 48' cruiser. There were, in all, twenty-four base models and near the middle of the runabout class could be found the 24' model 103. The "103" typified all the qualities of speed, style and grace inherant in the modern "speedboat" of the day. Capable of 35 mph with her standard 125 h.p. engine, the "103" could carry 10 passengers in her double forward and single aft cockpit. The price was $2,850.00 F.O.B. Alyonac, Michigan.

Mahogany runabouts of all makes are today a highly sought after item by antique and classic boat enthusiasts and an original 1930 model "103" even in a sad state of disrepair can cost more than it did when it was new. Add to this the labor costs of a professional restoration plus the time and care needed to keep the finished product in top shape and clearly the result is something to be enjoyed by someone with more than a few bucks in their boating budget.

However, more and more Americans today than ever before are reaching into the past to capture items that reflect a certain functional style and beauty somehow absent from current models. When demand nears or exceeds supply the modern reproduction steps in to fill the void. Reproductions in the field of Antique and Classic Automobiles have been around for some time. Marine reproductions are relatively new. Reproductions in any area can be a customer rip-off perpertrated by those strickly after the big bucks and nothing more, or they can be sincere and faithful works of art created by those whose skill and conscience will allow them to produce nothing but the very best.

One day earlier this spring while visiting Irwin Marine in Lakeport, NH, the local ChrisCraft dealer and perhpas the largest in the Northeast, I was pleased to find an example which falls into this latter category. There in the middle of the showroom was a gleaming, new 24-foot Grand-Craft mahogany runabout which is the modern reproduction of the 1930 ChrisCraft model 103. Only a handful of these boats will be produced this year, however Macatawa Bay Boat Works of Holland, Michigan has plans for more of the same plus other models in the future.

The Grand-Craft is the brainchild of a young marine engineer by the name of Steve Northuis who throughout his career in the boating industry has touted the use of wood for modern boats which in this age of mass-produced fiberglass and aluminum, met very little interest. However Northuis had more than a passing interest in the classic mahogany ruanbout and ~~had~~ has gained considerable knowledge in restoring many of these old boats. The answer, of course, was his own company and as his home state of Michigan had always been a prime mover in the industry qualified help would be close at hand. The term "qualified help" proved to be vastly underated in view of the men who ultimately joined Northuis in his venture. Chris Smith, grandson of the founder of ChrisCraft and his brother George, both recently retired became interested in the project. Subsequently other ChrisCraft retirees all with thirty-odd-years of experience joined to build the first Grand-Craft. What group could have been better qualified for the job.

The results are what all reproductions should strive to be: Classic preservations of the past coupled with a touch of non-distracting modern technology. As great as they were, the originals weren't perfect and afterall we have learned a couple things in the past fifty years. A modern 350 cubic inch, 255 H.P. ChrisCraft power plant tops the list. Next is a hull which is said to be 2½ times stronger than the original, this being accomplished by an inner hull of top grade marine plywood on which is fastened the mahogany planking with the whole assembly heavily treated with preservatives. Also, added ribs have been placed in the bow. The resulting hull is much more rigid than the original, vertually leakproof, and well able to stand the added horsepower. Authenticity is there where it counts; in the look, feel, and ride of the boat. Deck hardware was cast from the original ChrisCraft patterns and every graceful line of the hull is as it should be.

The present day buyer can custom order the Grand, to suit their taste as could his grandfather in 1930, however the list of options read a little differently. Custom Inboard Show trailer, Dietrich Roadster top, Roll Top Entertainment Console, Tape Player AM/FM Stereo, VHF 55 channel Marine Radio, Diesel Engine, and so on. The price? Well that, of course will vary depending on what you choose for interior appointments and options, but let us say that the Grand-Craft is not inexpensive. However $2,850 was not cheap in 1930 and high cost has always been relative to how much you have to spend, so if you're thinking of a hand-crafted, high-quality boat such as the Grand-Craft, one shouldn't think about money.

****

Photo # 1   Ann-Marie Capenter -- 24' Grand-Craft at Irwin Marine, Lakeport, NH   Note: White slash up middle of photo is support column in showroom. Boat placement allowed no other angle.   MISSING

Photo # 2   Reproduced photo from a reprint of article in Feb. issue of Lakeland Boating, Steve Hilson Photo, as noted.

1922 Johnson Model "A"

In the post World War One recession of 1920 & 21 business was generally bad and for the Johnson Motor Wheel Co. the picture looked even worse. A year or two previously, the small two cycle, air cooled opposed two cylinder bicycle motor had sold quite well and the Johnson brothers Lou, Harry, and Clarence, together with brother-in-law Warren Conover had marketed 17,000 such units in little more than 3 years. However, at the dawn of the "soon to be" roaring twenties, competition grew rapidly as manufacturers strove to make financial hay in a sagging economy. After the war new companies had sprung to life like countless moths eager to share in the light of a still young motorized transportation industry, but for those firms building bicycle motors what illumination remained seemed to cast its glow more in the direction of those who built motorcycles and automobiles. In 1920 the Johnson motor wheel sold for $97.50 plus war tax. The price for two complete Johnson motor bikes was $140.00. However, the cost of a medium sized motorcycle had dipped alarmingly close to that figure and indeed Ford had announced a price of a mere $365.00 for its base model automobile. The Johnson Motor Wheel Co. faded gracefully from the picture and the Johnson clan pondered other business possibilities.

The Johnson's experience in designing and building 2 cycle gasoline engines actually went back quite a ways. In 1903 Lou and Harry, then in high school, designed and built a two cycle 3 HP engine to power their small boat down the Wabash River. A few years and many engines later found the brothers's expertise in the marine engine field very high among their peers.

In 1910 their interest rose skyward and they began to think about airplanes. The culmination of their efforts resulted in the first successful American monoplane which flew on August 8, 1911, piloted by Lou Johnson. Of course, every part of the aircraft was of Johnson design. The engine was a lightweight 60 HP 2 cycle V-4. The airframe was aluminum and the wings were of light wood structure. Today it is obvious to many experts that the Johnson monoplane was 25 years ahead of its time, but unfortunately

1

in 1911 it was not taken seriously by the more established aviation powers. Had it been, the industry as a whole might have arrived at its present station by a much easier and faster route. A model of the Johnson aircraft is on exhibit at the Smithsonian Institution and for those interested in more about the Johnson's adventures in the air a look at the September 1961 issue of Argosy would be well worthwhile.

On Easter Sunday March of 1913, a tremendous rain storm accompanied by a tornado struck Terre Haute, Indiana and near the center was the Johnson factory. Nearly everything was destroyed. By 1915 the Johnsons were back in business building high speed marine engines in four models. Two of the largest size, a V-12 2 cycle design weighing only 590 pounds but producing 180 HP found their way into a hull of brother Lou's creation named Black Demon III and placed a close second in a race held in Chicago behind Disturber III a famous race boat of the day.

However, getting back to 1920 and the demise of the motor wheel found the Johnsons wanting to get back on the water. The bicycle engine was a good design and the outboard motor industry was overdue for a good dose of creative engineering. Why not keep the basic components of the little opposed twin as they were and substitute water cooled cylinders for the finned air cooled ones? Surrounding the engine with the other necessary parts to make up the revolutionary lightweight outboard was a snap for the Johnsons.

Late in 1921 production began on the new outboard. At 35 pounds the new Johnson Light twin weighed half as much as the two horsepower models of some other competitors. It was the first American design to offer 360 degree pivoting and had the first reverse lock. Shortly after its introduction Johnson marketed the first cavitation plate as an option on the Light Twin

Johnson started numbering the Light Twin at number 501 and the first half dozen motors were reputed to be test engines which never left the factory. The serial number of the engine pictured here is 707 which represents the model A in its very early stages, however several earlier motors still exist. Although Johnson fielded a complete line of outboards of different horsepower by the late 1920s the model A started it all and was produced basically unchanged for several years. Thousands of "A"s were built and today it represents the most common outboard to be found of this vintage

Many model "A" Johnsons are still being used today, not only by those few who collect and restore them, but by many who simply have use for a small outboard. The simple truth is that with decent care those early Johnsons would last almost indefinitely and they are still one darn fine motor.

Specifications

Bore & Stroke	2" x 1-1/2"
Cubic Inches	9.42
Horsepower	2 @ 2250 RPM
Weight	35 lbs.
Price	$140.00

1946 Evinrude Big Four

The man stood in the kitchen doorway. "What in hell is that?" he asked, incredulous at the sight of the Big Four.

"That is an outboard motor". I calmly replied.

"It looks like a Volkswagon engine with no fins on it. I've never seen anything like that. It looks brand new."

"It's certainly not new, but it's in pretty decent condition. You must have led a very sheltered life."

"I've got a sixteen foot Starcraft with a 65 horse Merc on it", he remarked in his own defense.

"This thing would probably blow the doors off it" I said, putting my wrench down on the table.

"Hmmmm", he muttered, moving closer to the Evinrude without taking his eyes from it. "Where's the refrigerator?"

"Over there in the corner," I pointed. "It's white, stands about five feet high".

"What's the matter with it?"

"It makes weird noises and drips water on the floor."

"Hmmm", the guy repeated and ambled over toward the refrigerator. In doing so he had to pass by the door to the dining room.

"My God, this room in full of outboards!" he exclaimed, turning back to me, his mouth slacked a little to one side.

It's all right. I know," I said trying to reassure him. It was true enough. There were sixty old motors in the dining room. Not just in a big pile, you understand, but in neat rows on their interlocked OMC stands. The dining room motors were either restored or excellent originals.

"You collect these things or something?"

I nodded.

"Look at all that old brass, will you," he muttered. Just then the refrigerator emitted a high pitched whine followed by gurgling noises. "Hmmm", said the repairman and set his tool box on the floor.

I decided not to show him the attic or garage and particularly not the cellar. The cellar was full of outboards with scarcely enough room to squeeze in a work bench, drill press, and a couple lathes. The only signs of normalcy were a washer, dryer and freezer in one far corner. My wife had insisted on this and I had good-naturedly provided a narrow path through the outboards. My wife and I had made a separate deal concerning the dining room. I would remove the furniture and install the outboards and in turn she would write the room off her housecleaning list, these duties being transferred to me. Many times while on hands and knees, trying to maneuver my 6 foot frame through a forest of outboard stands I had pondered the advantages of this deal.

A short time before the appliance repairman had arrived I had moved the Big Four, stand and all into the kitchen to change the lower unit. Hopefully, we would both be finished our respective chores by the time Ann-Marie returned from grocery shopping.

With the exception of a monstrous five cylinder, radial engined outboard built in small numbers by Cross during the late 1920's, the Evinrude Big Four is the largest of the American antique outboards. Introduced in 1930 as a racing engine, the big 60 cu. in. four cylinder 4-60 as it was called was also available on an on again, off again basis in one of its many forms for the next two decades. During this period it remained the undisputed class "F" champion of outboard racing, a position it continued to hold until Mercury's six cylinder Mark 75H came on the scene in 1957.

During World War II Evinrude designed more rugged components around the same powerhead and the result was the famous Storm Boat motor which powered assault craft and other small military boats in both the Pacific and European theaters. The engine was further used to power emergency water pumps aboard ships and was credited with preventing more than one vessel from going to the bottom after sustaining severe damage from the enemy.

The 4-60 seemed to show up everywhere in those days and on the dirt tracks of America it served as the favorite power plant of midget race cars, a class that dominated American auto racing for years!

After the war Evinrude found that they had parts to build a great many more Storm Boat engines and so after replacing the rather complex mounting system with a conventional transom clamp and changing the color from olive drab to its more traditional dull aluminum, the Big Four was sold to the public in full military dress. For various reasons Evinrude did not really push the Big Four on the American boater who had gotten used to smaller, more civilized outboards featuring a rewind starter. The Big Four as an outboard for general consumption had become seriously outdated. First off, it was offered as a rope start model only. Furthermore, most people were not ready to handle 50 HP in the palm of their hand and when secured to the transom of one of the lighter weight shallow vee outboard hulls appearing after the war the results could be somewhat more than dangerous. In the late 1940s Evinrude was getting ready to re-enter the big engine field with its modern alternate firing Big Twin, but in the meantime it was clearly Evinrude's advantage to sell the remaining Big Fours plus military versions of the slightly smaller Speedifour and the 30 cu. in. Speeditwin. They were all great outboards, but they were the last of their breed.

The Big Four pictured here appears minus one of its military accoutrements; that being the lower unit which got changed that day on the kitchen table. The military unit, like the rest of the outboard, was built for rough use. It was thick walled and featured a heavy skeg plus two additional skegs which protruded horizontally from each side of the gear case thus protecting the big three bladed bronze prop from almost any obstacle. It was fine for bouncing off coral reefs on the way to an enemy beach, but the prewar Evinrude unit now on this engine, slices the water much more efficiently for those of us who can take the time to treat the Big Four in a more kindly fashion. The substitution of a high pitch two blade prop for the military wheel also goes a long way towards making this big outboard a 40 MPH plus motor when placed on a decent hull in the 14 to 16 foot range.

3

The Evinrude Big Four is an outboard that goes about its business of blasting you over the water in a straightforward, no nonsense manner. It is certainly not quiet and of course has no gear shift so when you crank that twist grip throttle open with one hand you best be hanging on to something with the other.

POSTSCRIPT:

My wife was not particularly pleased to find both the refrigerator and the Big Four partially disassembled with various parts of each lying about the kitchen. A further point of consternation was the fact that in unloading the contents of the refrigerator the appliance repairman, whose name was Joe, and myself had seen fit to empty several bottles of beer which we agreed would just get warm if left to set around on the shelf. Amazingly she had never heard that bottled beer deteriorates rapidly as it is subjected to repeated temperature changes and my claim that this particular stock had probably had enough of that sort of thing and therefore must be either consumed or thrown away fell on deaf ears.

Fortunately for both of us we were able to purchase another home a couple of years ago. It is out of town, features attached sheds and a large barn on several acres of land. After taking nearly a month to move, my wife and I entered into another deal. Actually, it was not so much a deal as it was a simple straightforward statement uttered by my wife in clear tones, using perfect diction.

"There will be no outboard motors allowed in the house!"

Specifications

Type	4 cylinder opposed
Bore & Stroke	2.75" x 2.5"
Cubic Inches	59.9
Horsepower	50 @ 5500 RPM
Weight	178 lbs.
Price	$575.00

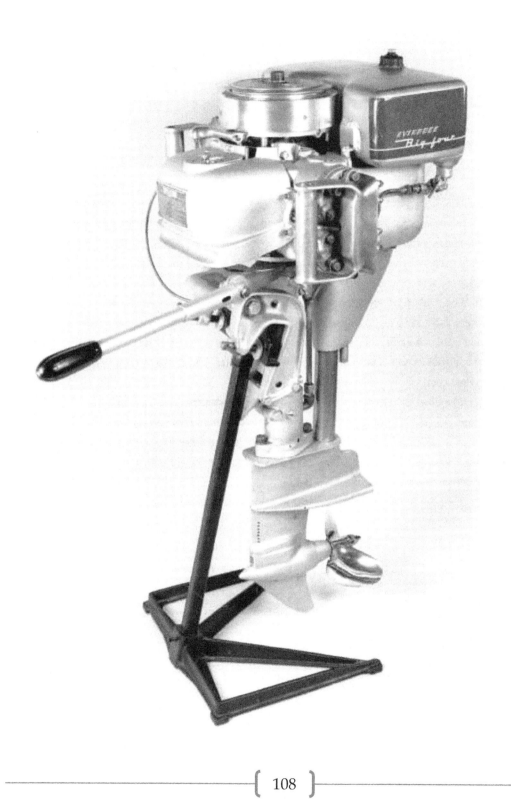

1914 Waterman Model C-14X

The name Waterman today, holds little significance to most modern outboarders, however concerning outboard heritage this name marks a number of firsts. Waterman was the first maker to mass produce outboard motors, having marketed 3000 units in 1907. There were in fact other outboards before this date, but for the most part they were built in small numbers and distributed on a limited basis. Indeed, Waterman was the first to coin the word "outboard", although the term "rowboat motor" persisted among other companies for several years thereafter. During its production period from 1905 to 1917 Waterman was considered to be a "top of the line" item featuring the latest advances in engine technology.

The beginnings of the Waterman go back to 1903 when Cameron B. Waterman of Detroit was attending Yale Law School. As a senior having his studies pretty much under control, Waterman found time to involve himself in another sport which was just gaining a public foothold, that sport being motorcycling. As fall gradually gave way to a standard nasty New England winter, Waterman took the opportunity to bring his single cylinder machine into this room to give it some needed attention and possible overhaul to prepare it for service during the nest season. In the course of this activity Waterman clamped the motor to the back of a chair to see the results of his handiwork. As the engine came to life and ran beautifully, Waterman suddenly visualized the back of the chair as the stern of a small boat and further conjured up in his mind the necessary components needed to turn a propeller.

After graduating from college in the spring of 1904 Waterman returned to Detroit and barely took time to get married before starting serious work on what he had come to to think of as the Waterman "Outboard" or "Porto" motor. Initial efforts resulted in an awkward device comprised of a Curtiss motorcycle engine which drove the prop by way of a chain drive set-up. Waterman was encouraged, but realized that he would require professional help to see his venture a success. In almost the same breath he purchased a small factory to manufacture something that as yet did not exist.

Oliver Barthal, a production engineer, arrived to design a marketable model which appeared in 1906 as a vertical air cooled cylinder atop a crankcase which also housed the flywheel. Only a few dozen of these still ungainly units were produced and sold, however they worked well and Waterman was jubilant over several letters from satisfied customers. All indications pointed toward hundreds or even thousands of possible sales so in 1907 after exchanging the air cooled cylinder for a water cooled unit, production proceeded full speed ahead.

The 1914 Waterman pictured here is quite a different machine from the 1907 model. By this date nearly all outboards had settled on the same basic configuration of the forward mounted horizontal cylinder, however the Waterman carried this exercise out in grand style and these engines must be considered "classics" of this era. The C-14 is possibly the flashiest outboard ever produced. The cylinder base, transom clamps bracket and gas tank are painted black. The aluminum crank case is painted a dull aluminum and the rudder, steering bar and spark plug cover are painted aluminum. The flywheel rim is polished nickel plate. With the exception of the bright copper cylinder water jacket, all other parts are polished brass and bronze. A very striking piece of equipment.

The outboard is shown with its external coil, battery box and wiring harness; it being a battery ignition model. Waterman was among the first to use the underwater exhaust method as opposed to the more standard muffler of the period. The exhaust pipe on this engine serves an additional purpose, it being the pivot support of the rudder. The steering bar is also mounted on this exhaust pipe. The attached steering rope can be utilized in a variety of ways. It can be of the length as sown to be manipulated by someone sitting close to the engine or it may extend through a series of small pulleys located around the gunwhales so that the outboard can be steered from any place in the boat.

2

Another item worthy of mention is the carburetor which in the case of the Waterman is really a carburetor and not a mixing valve as was used by most other manufacturers of the period. This particular Kingston carb incorporates a float regulated gas supply and is known as the five ball type. These live metal balls are located in the air intake passageway and rise off their seats to allow more or less air into the engine as RPM's demand.

Waterman outboards today are not common, but they are not considered rare when compared with several other makers of the same vintage. Their value is somewhat higher than most other brands, however keep in mind that old outboards are not a highly prized item when compared across the board with say, stationary engines, which have a much larger following with relatively fewer engines in existence. Speculators in the field of antique outboards may well be disappointed in the years to come.

Postscript: We hope to give the 1907 Waterman the once over here in this column sometime in the future after it receives a full restoration.

SPECIFICATIONS

Type	single cylinder
Bore 7 Stroke	2-3/4" x 3"
Cubic inches	17.81
Horsepower	3 @ 1000 RPM
Weight	59 lbs
Price	$82.00

1930 Johnson Model P-50

Looking back over the history of any mass produced item often induces a quick smile when the viewer sees what was pleasing to the eye way back when. Manufactured items of almost any description from an automobile to a toaster have always been built to incorporate a certain aesthetic style in their appearance. In the beginning the function of an object more often dictates its basic design, but as time goes by the stylist gets into the act and naturally sees fit to disguise mechanical workings. The results can be simple or fancy, tasteful or ostentatious and in some cases just plain confusing to the consumer. At the other extreme is the product that seems to revel in the job it does. Its' special features, it's' controls and indeed its' very guts are there for all to see because people are still getting a kick out of operating it for its' own sake and take a special delight in the way it works. This phase of evolution nearly always occurs when a product is still new and fresh in the minds of the public. As time passes and one becomes solely interested in the reliability of what it does rather than how it works, it is time to call in the stylists to cover up the mechanism and paint it pretty colors.

One further note on the evolution of style before I wear the subject out completely is that a fickle public can get bored with prettiness and yearn to return to the look of function, at least to some degree. A good example is the new breed of four wheel drive pickup trucks seen cruising the nation's highways in increasing numbers. It sports huge tires that look like they came off a payloader and its whole chassis is jacked up another foot off the ground. It appears like some wild beast and probably sounds like one. It's FWD and its' functional capability is right there in plain sight. It could probably climb tall buildings if it wanted to. On the other hand, that same truck may well have a $2000. paint job, so it never strays very far from a paved surface where a tree branch might scratch its' finish. Oh well, function is only popular as long as it's in style.

In the history of the outboard motor perhaps no other engine has exhibited that school of raw-bones design of pure mechanical purpose as did that new breed of outboard brought forth by Johnson during 1929 and 30. The model P-50 also known as the Seahorse "24" shown here is a prime example.

Some time ago a friend of mine came upon a P-50 gathering dust in the cellar of a house in which he was installing a new furnace. As the cellar was slated to become a playroom in the near future the owners asked my friend John if he would care to dispose of several unwanted items, the old Johnson being one of them. John, a very intense small boating freak hereabouts became extremely excited at the prospect of cruising down the lake with this old relic and lost no time in hauling it home that very noon. Proudly displaying his find in the back of his truck to his wife and 5 year old son, John found their reactions somewhat less than encouraging.

"Is that really an outboard motor?" his wife asked. "It looks like just a bunch of parts stuck together."

"Look Mommy, Daddy's outboard is throwing up," giggled John Jr.

John dismissed these comments in a typical chauvinistic manner and prepared to carry his cumbersome prize into the garage. While involved in this endeavor he tripped and fell, allowing the motor to land on his lower torso, causing a painful injury of a somewhat embarrassing nature, to be inflicted by one of the engine's many appendages. To this day, his wife, Brenda states that a curious imprint remains on his body. I among others have repeatedly requested to view this phenomenon, but to no avail. John's enthusiasm over the old Johnson diminished somewhat after this incident and immediate efforts towards restoration was further postponed when a cursory examination revealed that during its last outing long since forgotten, the engine had sought to rearrange some of its' internal parts in what must have been a very dramatic event. Needless to say theP-50 that appears here is a different one entirely.

The Johnson Seahorse "24" of 1930 represented the very latest in small engine technology. Where today such terms as electronic ignition and loop charging can be heard while perusing a dealer's showroom, in 1930 one listened to such things as rotary intake valves and release chargers. The class "C" or 30 cu. in. P-50 was not the largest engine Johnson offered that year, but its 20 HP did put it in the high mid-range category. The P-50 looks like it means business and it does, so let's take a quick look at the geography of this now very old looking outboard.

At the front of the powerhead can be seen the carburetor intake assembly and directly behind this, the choke lever. Proceeding toward the large open flywheel we come to the Vacturi carb, itself a very well designed unit which could be found on several different outboards over a period of two decades. Between the carburetor and the engine crankcase resides the rotary intake valve that meters the gas-air mix to the engine. The circular casting located directly beneath the spark advance lever houses the half speed (half crankshaft speed) gear which operates the valve itself in the intake manifold below.

The cylinders are offset on this motor to allow for straight connecting rods. This was also something new for Johnson in this engine configuration as earlier models had cylinders directly opposite each other necessitating bent rods. Higher RPMs and increased compression, dictated the straight rods. The cylinders also featured water cooled removable heads, a first in this model line. Attached to the port cylinder is a conglomeration of equipment, the tiller handle itself has a button on the tip which is the magneto kill switch. To the rear of the smooth cast aluminum handle is another webbed grip which is the throttle twist grip that works through a control wire looped underneath and around to the opposite side of the carb. The forward two-thirds of the tier swings upward to a vertical position, but this is a questionable convenience as the carburetor sticks out almost as far. Bolted to the port cylinder also is the compression release mechanism, a device started a year earlier on all Johnson base models, but carried a bit further in 1930. Pushing the lever toward the port spark plug depressed a spring loaded valve which released compression off this cylinder through a port in the head thus greatly reducing the effort needed to rope start the motor. In addition to this, a control rod near the lower part of the cylinder operated another valve which shut down all intake

3

gasses entering the port cylinder, thereby doubling or supercharging the starboard cylinder. Spark was also intensified to the starboard side. This, said Johnson, eliminated starting problems under adverse conditions. Once the engine started the lever was moved toward the flywheel and normal two cylinder operation was assumed.

To the rear of the powerhead and beneath the gas tank is located the large cast muffler which empties into the exhaust tube that carries exhaust gasses to the underwater outlet. Midway down the starboard side of this tube is yet another valve, exhaust pressure operated, which allows the exhaust to escape above the water at slow speeds or when the engine is being started, thus affording easier breathing. For better breathing at all speeds one could remove a large plate from the rear of the muffler and let it all hang out all the time. This was frequently done as the P-50 and its kind are not quiet engines under any circumstances. Progressing along these lines still further; the racing edition of this outboard had no exhaust system at all, but utilized stacks or simple deflectors bolted to the exhaust ports and turned in the neighborhood of 6000 RPM. In this configuration it is advised that a person apply some form of adequate ear protection else the noise will begin to chew up sizable chunks from ones sanity in a very short time.

Cooling the P-50 is handled quite nicely without the aid of a water pump. The propeller blades forces water into a duct which then is carried up through the powerhead and exhaust system by way of a network of cast in passageways and external piping.

Operating the P-50 can really be a lot of fun, although at first one must keep their mind on what they are doing. The spark and gas controls are not synchronized so this will require both hands and a little thought throughout the full RPM range. Then too, if the engine is clamped on the stern of a fairly light boat one has to watch where they are going while operating the motor because they are going to be traveling in the 30 MPH range at full throttle. Besides the exhaust noise, which is after all not that horrendous at planing speeds with a stock engine, the P-50 sounds about like it looks. One can hear every separate engine sound, the air rushing into the carb, the whine of the gear operated rotary valve, and so forth. As you look at the engine with those things seemingly sticking out all over it you certainly have a clear impression of what's going on in there. One can find themselves really liking the experience if they're a little weird to begin with and who among us isn't?

The rotary valve Johnson "P" series that started in 1930 was manufactured with only minor refinements for the twenty years through 1950 which speaks highly for its basic design and ruggedness. It, along with the comparable Evinrude Speeditwin were the last of their opposed engine breed to be produced in this country, surprising in itself when one remembers that Johnson was the first to introduce a line of alternate firing in-line twins the same year the P-50 was unveiled.

The most common of the "P" series to be found today is the PO-15 which is the last model designation and was manufactured from 1941 until the "P" stopped altogether. After WWII they were painted that same old Johnson green used until the mid 1950s that many people are still familiar with.

The stock prop on all models is a 12" x 12" three blade bronze wheel which gives a surprising acceleration and good load carrying power. So if you happen to run across an old Johnson "P" while poking around the inner depths of some marina or anywhere else at all, (old outboards can be found in the darnedest places) stop and give the old girl a second glance. Old model "Ps" are not a particularly valuable item so for little or nothing and possibly a little tinkering an old "P" may still have a thrill or two left somewhere deep inside.

Heck, you may even find one in your cellar. Just be extra careful while you're carrying it around.

5

ANTIQUE CORNER

by

Lawrence C. Carpenter

1957 Bucaneer 12 HP

and a furtive glance into the world of the outboard collector

To one who has more than a passing interest in outboard motors, the mid to late 1950's can often produce a yawn. Outboards of this period and onward are viewed as contemporary in nature and tend to blend together in a kaleidoscope of multicolored engine shrouds. Admittedly there have been numerous refinements over the past couple of decades, not the least of which is a considerable improvement in the area of gas consumption. To some of those big motors of the sixties the standard six gallon tank served only as an appetizer.

However, very little research has been done to determine the nature of the disease that attacks the outboard collector, although the fact that we are dealing with a functional malady can be firmly attested to by the wives of those so afflicted. Symptoms can vary with the individual. Eyes can become wide and develop a fixed stare while gazing at an open flywheel. Hands may become wet and clammy at the touch of the nickel plated cylinders of any early Elto Quad. One poor soul was found to exhibit a perverted fascination for naked sparkplugs pointing in opposite directions. The resulting ailment can often leave one totally useless around the house, or so wives claim.

Many collectors have been known to get out of bed in the middle of the night and drive a hundred miles as the result of a phone call indicating the availability of a particular outboard. Family members frequently notice strange terms or phrases creeping into the speech of the outboarded victim. One husband, after being forced to discuss family affairs while polishing a gas tank was heard to respond angrily to his wife,

"I think your mother has lost a blade off her prop!".

For every outboard collector there are several "therapists" trying to get him back on the straight and narrow. Such therapists are quite easy to come by since the only credentials they require are a complete disinterest in outboards and possibly a distaste for bodies of water large enough to float a boat. The first thing a practicing therapist does in determining the seriousness of the condition of his targeted "collector patient" is to look at his collection. This can give valuable clues as to the roots of the illness and indicate possible treatment. The man who is found to have in his possession a dozen or so motors with only a few of an age of questionable utility, can usually be talked out of his dilemma without having to endure severe withdrawal pains. However, when viewing a collection of early rowboat motors or "knuckle busters" of the teens, the therapist will laugh long and hard hoping to shame the collector into dislodging himself of these useless artifacts. This approach seldom works and usually only serves to drive the subject deeper into his shell. The life of a therapist can be dangerous to his own mental well being unless he is careful. He may, while on call, find himself inside a large building filled with hundreds of outboards of all ages, shapes and sizes just laying there lurking in the gloom. The mere touch of an ancient grease-laden lower unit in the darkness can make his blood run cold and cause the therapist to run screaming from the premises, while it is the collector who laughs uncontrollably at the departing figure as he crouches in the midst of his domain, dripping saliva and clutching his favorite old racing engine. Like alcoholics, old outboard collectors have become crafty in the denial of their problem.

"But my dear, I am, or at least I used to be, a dealer. I just don't feel right without a few outboards around."

"Honey, you wouldn't make me throw away Dad's old outboards and the dozen or so parts motors I've found to keep them going, would you?"

The old outboard collector must never plead or otherwise demean himself. The smart collector who plans well in advance will take steps to shield himself from do-gooders and present a picture of normalcy to the outside world. One popular action is the acquisition of a few outboards built in the late 1950's or early sixties. Though these motors are sometimes of little interest in themselves to the collector they can help to legitimize an entire collection of what the untrained eye may see as so much worthless iron. These more contemporary motors are still highly useful, can be had for nominal prices and make a great deal of sense. Furthermore, a practicing collector should be able to justify acquiring engines throughout the entire horsepower range and a scenario toward this end might go like this.

"No finer fishing motors can be had at any price than these little Johnson and Evinrude 3 HP alternate twins of the fifties," the collector tells his wife who quickly nods as if listening to a judgemental decree. "And one will fit nicely in the car trunk this spring when we go camping in Death Valley. This little Fleetwin here will be just the thing for the kids, -- er when we have some and when they get a little older this 10 HP Merc is going to be great! Moving on to the mid range engines I've got this electric starting 1957

Evinrude Fastwin. Isn't it a beauty? This will be your motor. Its just the right size. And then just a little bigger is this smooth running Mark 28A. Of course, I don't ever want to have to change a water pump in one of these things so I've got a couple more standing by. Moving on quickly here past our old friend, the Johnson 25, and skipping over this classic Oliver 35 we come to this pair of three-cylinder Flying Scotts. These babies will pull our whole family on water skis with a few neighbors coming along for the ride. But keep in mind that McCullochs are hard to find parts for so I've got these other engines........er, then we come to this here West Bend Tiger Shark -- 80 vicious horsepower. Say, these motors were rare then, and someday this thing is going to be worth ....".

This particular old outboard collector hasn't been paying attention. He suddenly realizes that the look he is now getting from his wife is altogether different from the one he remembers only moments ago. All at once he knows! Like a needle, a sharp shiver of fear pierces the consciousness of the collector. She's not buying any of it, he thinks. She doesn't believe a word! He finds that he has averted eye contact with his spouse and is now looking at the floor of his garage where his car used to be, but that was long ago before the outboards. He is visibly shaken now and within seconds is suffering a total uncontrollable breakdown. A once proud outboarder has degenerated into a simpering mass, a spineless wimp.

I am embarrassed. Unknowingly I picked a weakling to illustrate this critical point. There will be no therapists for this guy. Why waste the time? There's no need. His motors will all be gone by the end of the month. The poor slob! I hasten to add that the vast majority of us are made of sterner stuff and could have carried this off with no problem.

The number of those who collect outboards is still quite small, so although the disease of outboard-mania may reach epidemic proportions within the hobby it remains little more than a nuisance to the nation as a whole. With the absence of a national campaign to combat the illness, family members find themselves without leadership and must continue to curse the darkness individually. Bad for them. Good for us. Indeed in most localities wives must call long distance to console one another.

The Bucaneer outboard pictured here was manufactured by Gale Products of Galesburg Ill., a division of Outboard Motors Corporation. Gale was also responsible for the production of several "private brand" outboards which were built under contract for other companies to be marketed through their own outlets. A couple examples are the Sea King, manufactured by Gale for Montgomery Ward & Co. and the SeaBee, built for Goodyear Tire and Rubber Co. Gale built other private brands as did almost every other major outboard manufacturer of this period.

Although the practice of private brand outboards was started back in 1914 when Lockwood-Ash put together an outboard called the Motorgo and sold it to Sears-Roebuck, the 1950's saw the greatest proliferation of these motors. Indeed during this decade more outboard motors were sold in this country than all previous years combined.

Although sold through its own dealership network the Bucaneer which fielded a complete range of outboards was identical to private brand motors built by Gale except for name, minor trim, and color. The statement that private brands were put together from parts that were factory "seconds" of the parent company is not well-founded, particularly where engine and drive line components were concerned.

However, slightly outdated parts were used to build outboards that in some cases were intended to be a more stark and basic machine than top-of-the-line motors. But a smaller price tag also went along with these engines that all in all stood up very well to the competition in the areas of quality and durability. Nevertheless, OMC and Mercury took other steps to insure that one of their private brand motors would not compete directly against their own lineup that had retained the same size powerhead for several years. Through a slightly downsized cylinder bore the private brand engine had a little less displacement than the parent model. Hence this Bucaneer has a displacement of 17.89 cubic inches. The Evinrude Fastwin displacement is 19.94.

Other smaller outboard manufacturers such as Scott Atwater and Champion didn't get quite so basic in order to foil model for model competition by their own private brand engines, probably for reasons of expense. These makers were apt to use simpler methods to downrate their poorer cousins and oftentimes these measures could be reversed by clever outboarders.

This particular 12 HP Bucaneer is as close to a mint condition original as one can hope to get except for the occasional old outboard still in its factory packing case. This engine was found to have been run perhaps half an hour. The green paint is still shiny and unfaded inside the exhaust outlet. Although this is a manual start model, the same outboard could be ordered with electric starting which together with its other features certainly put it on equal footing with the 15 HP Johnson or Evinrude Fastwin except for its slightly smaller powerhead.

This outboard makes a lot of practical sense, even today and together with several other engines of the late 1950's and early 60's proclaims to one and all that I feel just fine; have nothing in the way of a bad habit; and posses an uncommonly healthy outlook on life.

Specifications

Engine Type	Alternate Firing Twin
Bore & Stroke	2 1/4" x 2 1/4"
Cubic Inches	17.89
Horsepower	12 @ 4000 RPM
Weight	75 lbs
Shift	Forward, Neutral, Reverse
Fuel	6 Gal. auxiliary tank
Cost	$365.00

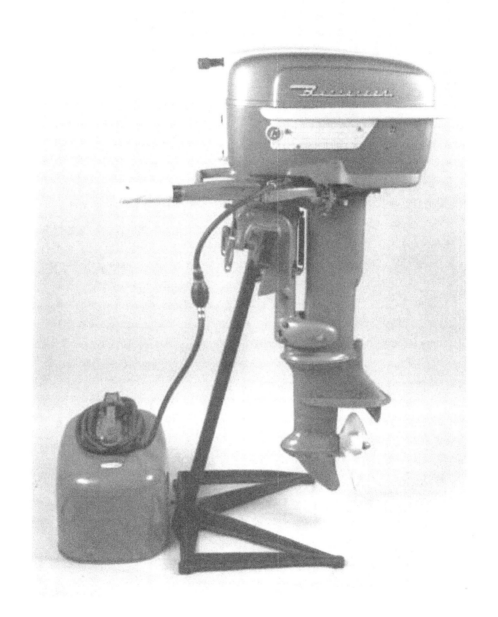

The Original Skiboard

A half century ago the world of pleasure boating was still in the midst of an upheaval which had started only in few years earlier. One of the main elements of this changing scene was the introduction of speed in large doses to craft from one end of the boating spectrum to the other. Near the top of the line was a type of boat which became known as the "commuter". Although today this term is more commonly applied to a tiny car that scurries about the inner city sipping gas by the spoonful; the commuter of the thirties took the form of a huge mahogany speedboat of thirty to fifty feet or more in length powered by multiple engines sometimes totaling over 1000 horsepower and capable of over 50 MPH. These hulls featured cabins of the express cruiser type and were appointed with all the latest luxuries to please and pamper its occupants, be they one or two dozen. Perhaps the greatest concentration of these boats built by Hacker, GarWood, Chris Craft Dodge and others was to be found streaking down Long Island Sound on any given weekday morning as they transported a bank president, corporation head or other wealthy individual from his estate on the island to his office in Manhattan. Their operation was of course completely handled by a chauffeur-captain and crew enabling the owner to contemplate the day's business ahead or maybe enjoy racing a fellow executive to the city. Needless to say gas consumption was not a major consideration of this latter day commuter.

On the other end, or perhaps the bottom end, if your scale is in dollars, of the boating spectrum was the outboard motor. It hadn't been that long since an outboard had pushed a boat out of the water to achieve a firm planing attitude and the result proved a source of endless enjoyment for those involved with these small marine powerplants. As the popularity of outboards increased, people sought new ways to put them to use. Some of the contraptions that found their way from the backyard workshop to the waters edge quickly realized their usefulness was very short lived; however pictured here is a little craft that proved quite successful and managed to survive with one or two refinements until the early sixties.

The little boat in question or rather the oversized aquaplane shown here was developed during the late twenties almost as soon as there were outboards built powerful enough to push it along on a fast plane. It was called the skiboard. Anywhere from six to eight feet in length the skiboard was a fully encapsulated structure, square on each end, with a flat bottom and a turned up nose. Its flotation capabilities were barely enough to handle an outboard of up to 14 HP weighing perhaps 70 to 80 lbs. clamped to its raised transom and one adult of either gender. For controlling one's position on the speedy little craft one had only a rope secured to the forward corners of the skiboard in aquaplane fashion and for steering you simply shifted your weight from side to side. Very little is said concerning throttle control of the craft, particularly during its early use and in the accompanying photos no throttle control device is really evident. One method was simply to reach back and attempt to regulate the outboard in a normal manner, however this was awkward at best. Hand held crash type throttles were tried, but the beginner usually preferred to have both hands on the rope and the veteran game player needed one hand free as I'll touch upon later. Another speed control method was a foot or rather an ankle operated device that left the ball of the foot free to keep balance but allowed a pivoting motion of the ankle to put pressure on a spring loaded bar raised slightly off the deck and located along one side of the craft. Connected to a throttle cable, the length of the bar offered throttle control from a variety of rider positions bow to stern. A spring returned throttle or a magneto cut off switch attached to some portion of the rider's body by way of a string served to halt the craft in case said rider took an unscheduled dive into the water. Such a precaution although not always used, guarded against a skiboard going on its merry way by itself to smash into the shore or other craft or possibly carve up swimmers with the prop although protective devices encircling the propeller were used during competitive games.

It was said that mastering the skiboard was much easier than it looked and judging by the number of people involved in the sport at one time, this is probably true. Skiboards could be purchased from several different manufacturers for 50 to 60 dollars or constructed by the amateur boat builder from plans available at the time.

The most popular game associated with the skiboard was the sport of water polo which gained national attention through its development in of all places, Texas. This was accomplished through the efforts of a Dr. J. A. Hockaday of Port Isabel and some leagues and teams were formed in various parts of the United States. Water polo rules were loosely fashioned after its dry counterpart with a few necessary equipment modifications, notably the use of a larger floating ball and mallets with hollow heads to afford less water resistance when swinging at it.

Prime movers in the Florida area, another water polo stronghold, included such notables as Malcolm Pope, the most famous outboard stunt driver of the time and perhaps the primary individual responsible for the development of water skiing and boat jumping along with being a top outboard racer for more than two decades.

Water polo, at least in this form has long since faded from the scene, however the skiboard survived with a measured popularity until the 1960's where at such point the support rope was replaced with a rigid upright structure to afford the rider a better chance to keep his or her balance and also provide a place to mount engine controls. Who knows? A few may still be around.

When looking at the fads that were popular way back when it's easy to assume a look of wistful appreciation for the good old days, but if one takes a minute to review today's boating scene with it's jet skis and wet bikes its plain to see that people don't change; the equipment does!

1950 Mercury Model KG-7H Hurricane Class "B" Racing Engine

Long before World War II came to an end major American outboard manufacturers were planning ahead to the day they could once again enter the consumer market. Outboard makers like the automotive industry had been heavily involved in the war effort and had all but suspended production of consumer items, however it was clear to all that peacetime would bring instant demand for these products and the company that could offer something new to the public could expect a head start on the competition.

Although, under the banner of Outboard Motors Corporation, Johnson and Evinrude were still viewed as separate companies and produced competing lines of totally different motors. Both had manufactured military versions of outboards of all horsepowers and being locked into this activity, found it impossible to put on a completely new face in 1946. Evinrude, particularly found its line of opposed twins and fours severely outdated after the war although in the smaller horsepower ranges sold engines in great numbers, an example being the tiny four cylinder 5.4 HP Zephyr which still exists by the thousands. Though a fine outboard, this smallest of the four cylinder models grew expensive to build in the competitive post war market.

Johnson found itself in a somewhat better position from an engineering standpoint due to its experience with the alternate firing design concept it had pioneered in 1930. Two of Johnson's alternate twins in the 5 HP and under category became instant favorites. The 14 cu. in. "K" series was another story in that it had changed very little in the past 10 years and found itself sorely underpowered in the 10 HP class. Perhaps Johnson's most exciting outboard in 1946 was the "SD", a 22 cu. in. displacement, 16 HP alternate twin. This engine was designed just before the war and proved to be a powerhorse, although in 1951 when along with Evinrude, Johnson introduced it's completely new outboard lineup topped by the new 36 inch, 25 HP "RD" model, Johnson couldn't seem to find room for the"SD" and it was dropped. Maybe it had something to do with the fact that under light load conditions the difference in performance between the "SD" and the new "RD" was hardly worth mentioning.

Mercury was certainly not of the size of either Johnson or Evinrude n 1946, however for two basic reasons this young company may have been in the best position of all to take advantage of the post wear business boom and thereby capture a sizable chunk of the outboard market.

Reason number one was simply that Mercury, relatively new in the outboard field, was still formulating its own image and not being married to an existing product line could direct its efforts toward advanced designs. Indeed, shortly before the war the company had introduced such an outboard. Though its largest model was but an 11 cu. in, 6 HP engine, it was one of the most modern outboards of its day and a forecast of things to come.

Karl Kiekhaefer was a brilliant design engineer, well versed in metallurgy and the creation of special machine tools. He was also an excellent business man and in 1939 his ambition led him to purchase the Cedarsburg Manufacturing Corporation of Cedarsburg, Wisconsin which had built and marketed the Thor outboard since 1934. Thors were relatively crude but innovative machines and at the time of Kiekaefer's purchase the plant was in the midst of a contract with Montgomery Ward, a contract that was to supply outboards which they would sell under their brand name, Sea King. Carl Kiekaefer had not given much thought to the outboard motor as such, but among the company assets he had just purchased were a great many Thor outboards which had remained as rejects. Kiekaefer thought the Montgomery Ward contract should be filled and besides it offered immediate business for his new firm. However he could not bring himself to allow these motors to leave the premises even had they been up to Thor standards. It was obvious to his trained eye and creative mind that they could be improved in several areas.

When the shipment was finally made the outboards Montgomery Ward received were far superior than their predecessors and orders poured in for more. Carl Kiekaefer gave some more serious thought to the outboard at that time. True, these small machines were far removed from his original intentions, but in his brief involvement he had become fascinated with the possibilities they presented. Carl Kiekaefer became hooked on outboards and the first of his own "Mercurys" was soon built.

In February of 1942 the War Production Board Limitation Order No. 80 issued by the federal government stopped all manufacturing of outboard motors for public sale and the industry turned its any talents toward the war effort. Mercury was no exception. Kiekaefer Corp. did not have a complete line of outboards to offer the military as did OMC, so the company took a different course than did its larger competitor and herein lies that second reason mentioned earlier. Kiekaefer launched a crash program geared toward the development of powerful lightweight two cycle engines in many configurations and sizes. Square and opposed fours, V-twins and fours, radials, and two, three and four cylinder in-line models up to 90 HP were engineered and built. Some of these engines powered pumps, generators, chainsaws, compressors, target aircraft and a host of other equipment for the military. By the wars end Kiekaefer Corp. had become one of the leading authorities on two cycle engines in the world and when it became time to turn once again to the outboard motor Mercury possessed a wealth of knowledge from which to draw and the company lost no time in putting it to good use.

The first post war models were similar to those produced in 1941 as Mercury continued to build engines for the military, but for 1947 the company brought forth the Lightning model. This 20 cu. in. outboard rated at 10 HP was an instant success. One of the original "green" Mercs, its streamlined powerhead casing is still not seriously outdated even by today's standards. Post war outboaders were quick to realize that this superbly designed and quality built motor would easily surpass its 4000 RPM rating enabling the lightning to seriously challenge outboards much larger than itself. Mercury broadened its outboard line up and sale skyrocketed. In 1949 the model KF-9

Thunderbolt was introduced. The worlds first four cylinder in-line outboard, this 40 cu. in. engine rated at 25 HP put Mercury firmly into a position of leadership in the big motor field, a position which it has held through most of its existence.

In 1950 the Lightning powerhead was replaced with the now famous Hurricane engine. The same size as the Lightning, the Hurricane made the 10 HP rating seem ludicrous and Mercury, not one to push its power ratings, finally added a "plus" after the figure 10. Indeed, when compared to other makers, the Hurricane would come close to producing nearly double its advertised horsepower in stock form. Mercury was well established as a "fast" outboard and the Hurricane served to only strengthen these beliefs. Further proof was evidenced with the introduction of the model KG-9, successor to the KF, still rated at 25+ HP. but producing close to 40. It was perhaps the fastest outboard motor to reach the American outboarder up until that time.

Outboard racing was a major influence in popularizing the outboard during the mid to late twenties and manufacturers spent a great deal of money sponsoring and promoting races, speed and endurance events, racing teams, etc. After the stock market crash in 1929 these companies found it impossible to continue such activities although they still built racing engines to be bought and used by individuals.

In 1931 the racing commission of the newly formed National Outboard Association formulated an agreement which was approved by the major outboard companies. In essence this pact allowed these companies to collectively withdraw from subsidizing the racing scene thus saving themselves large sums of cash, but it also prohibited the same concerns from benefiting from race results through advertising. The general thought at the time was that racing had done its job in promoting the outboard to the boating public and although racing itself might suffer, overall outboard sales would not. As things turned out racing did not suffer at all, but continued to grow throughout the thirties.

During the war racing in any real sanctioned form came to a halt. Manufacturers were not building outboards anyway and most people had more important things on their mind. At war's end another factor served to dampen the spirit of the racing fraternity still further. OMC, now Evinrude and Johnson, decided not to resume building racing engines. It didn't make sense for the company to race against itself and besides time and resources would best be spent satisfying the post war market as a whole.

As for the outboard racer himself, the roar of the open exhausts while cutting through a leaders roostertail on the way to that final turn was not easily forgotten and in back yards and garages across the country pre-war racing outboards could be heard sputtering to life. Racers, grinned broadly as they dusted off their old equipment. Parts proved hard to come by and racers had to scrounge for needed items in order to gain that elusive competitive edge. War surplus pumps and military outboards provided a source of powerheads to be carefully disassembled, polished and balanced by the racer. Speciality companies sprang to life almost overnight to build lower units as well as other parts needed to keep these old engines running. Boat manufacturers carefully eyed the resurgence of outboard racing as new builders brought their sleek new hulls to the race course.

Carl Kiekaefer was also well aware of these goings on and a decision was made. Mercury stepped through the open door of outboard racing and for all practical purposes slammed it shut in the face of OMC for years to come

Racing provided an added impetus for Mercury as engines such as the racing model pictured in this column came to dominate the sport in a relatively short time. This particular engine is a restored example of the breed and represents one of the finest outboard engines every built. The KG-7H remains a thing of beauty with its streamlined powerhead and "quicksilver" racing lower unit. Perhaps it appearance here will tug at the heartstrings of many an old outboard racer.

5

Specifications

Engine type	alternate firing twin
Bore & Stroke	2-7/16" x 2-1/8"
Cubic Inches	19.8
Horsepower	20+, depending on RPM
Weight	65 lbs.
Cost	$400.00
Top Speed	50+ MPH

1948 Old Town 14' Square Stern Rowboat

The Old Town Canoe Co. is one of the nation's oldest boat builders and as its name implies is most famous for the thousands of canvas covered cedar strip canoes it has built over the years. These slender craft are still being built by Old Town as people all over the country seem to have rediscovered the fact that canoeing on lakes and streams can be exhilarating as well as relaxing and many of these people find they prefer the look and feel of the traditionally built wood canoe although Old Town builds the fiberglass model for those who demand that their fun be made from modern materials.

The fact that Old Town built other type hulls is not remembered by many, but indeed during the first half of this century the variety of boats being constructed in Old Town, Maine included rowboats of several different styles, flashy, fully equipped runabouts, stepped hydroplanes for family fun or competition, as well as their extensive lineup of canoes. The vast majority of these boats were of cedar strip construction, however the Old Town pictured here is of a different breed entirely. The Old Town company didn't see fit to build a boat using the lapstrake construction method until the early thirties, but once breaking the ice they continued a relatively small line of these hulls until the mid 1950's when the wood boat market began to face hard times.

This model began its existence as one of Old Town's original examples and remained unchanged through the late 1940's. One of two basic rowboat styles, the "square stern" was designed to accommodate outboards up to the twelve horsepower range a well as possess excellent rowing characteristics which the finely cast bronze oarlocks - or more correctly, rowlocks will testify to. The boat's length was listed as fourteen feet, however this dimension was measured along the gunwhales as were most boats of the day. True straight line length, transom to bow, is about six inches less. The graceful lines of this cedar planked and oak framed hull are quite evident, however one interesting feature hidden here should be touched upon. Old Town realized long ago that even a mid range outboard, after pounding a hull such as this over wave upon wave could be responsible for causing a keel to take on a concave set after a few short years of use, thus badly effecting its handling, therefore Old Town raised its already substantial outboard keel to a height of about four inches to strengthen the tender midsection of the hull from a point about one foot forward of the transom until it tapered back to normal exposure halfway to the bow. The result also produced exceptional directional stability.

Back when this boat was built, wood of course, was the primary marine building material and builders did not exactly fool around as the construction record of this particular hull will show. This grade AA "square stern" was completely built on June 8th 1948. It was fitted on the 9th and was stained and varnished on the 10th. It received a second coat of varnish on the 14th and was shipped on the 17th. Not bad for the leisurely good old days.

The boat remains in remarkably good condition as this recent photo illustrates and would only require only very minor wood attention and a new finish to be absolutely mint. Further, it is amazing that at sometime over the years someone didn't decide to take a popular shortcut to proper upkeep and slop a coat of paint on it, but alas this hull has managed to receive additional varnish as needed to preserve its clear natural finish.

While on the subject of older wood boats, I would like to take a book review stance to mention a new book on the scene which to my knowledge is the most extensive volume ever compiled on small wood boats. It is Volume IV in the Real Runabout series by Bob Speltz. Referred to as the Outboard Edition, this massive 590 page work deals also with canoes and rowboats as well as every conceivable outboard powered type hull. It contains 2000 photographs, details all construction methods of the wood hull and traces the history of hundreds of wood boat builders. Also present is a section on outboard motors past and present, another concerning model boats and motors, and more. At $55.00 postpaid it is expensive, but well worth the money and a must for anyone interested in these subjects. The book is available from the AOMC Store, RD2, Box 33C, Unadilla, NY 13849. Incidentally you will find this little Old Town on page 253.

2

Antique Corner

by

Lawrence Carpenter

SCOTT-ATWATER 1946-1957

Cruising slowly along beside the public docks at Weirs Beach, N.H. in July, I finally spotted a space large enough to accomodate the fifteen foot Yellow Jacket. As I neared the dock I noticed a man and his wife standing there as if saving the space for someone else. While staring in my direction, the man displayed a look of obvious displeasure and I glanced around to see if another boat intended to claim my mooring. There was no one. First come, first serve, I thought and gently clunked the big Scott into reverse and jabbed the throttle to bring the boat to a stop. The outboard responded with a low throaty roar from its dual exhaust not unlike the sound emitted from the two glass-packed mufflers of a fifties Lincoln I had owned years before.

"That's not the same motor. It can't be!" I heard the wife exclaim as I reached for the dock. I looked up to see her holding on to her husband's arm as if restraining him from some possible violent action and judging by the expression on the man's face, it was plain to see that he was very angry indeed. I stood up straight and looked at them both, warily waiting to learn what the problem was. The man, however, was not concerned with me at all. He had yet to take his eyes from the 1955 30 H.P. Scott-Atwater on the stern of the Yellow Jacket.

"Ralph, I tell you it's not the same one!" The wife pulled on Ralph"s arm as if to get his attention. "You____you destroyed it a long time ago."

Carpenter

"Somehow it has survived", Ralph uttered through clenched teeth. "Somehow it has managed to return."

Ralph hadn't noticed my existence, but finally his wife did. I had begun to think I was watching the Twilight Zone. "We_____we used to have one of those." she said, forcing a sidewards glance at the outboard, then flashing an apologetic smile at me. "It_____it didn"t work very well." I nodded sympathetically. Ralph was still muttering to himself.

"Now that you've shut it off, I'll bet it won't start!" Ralph had noticed me at last and appeared no less upset at my having brought this mechanical apparition into his midst. I resumed a sitting position behind the wheel and smiled sweetly at Ralph as I touched the starter. The gleaming green and gold Scott-Atwater settled into a rumbling idle as its exhaust bubbled noisily at the transom. Ralph was livid. I backed the Yellow Jacket away from the dock and began searching for a safer location to put the boat. I had to assume that this guy could be dangerous to the welfare of the old Scott. For a moment I contemplated moving the outboard to the confines of my bedroom closet untill these people left town.

Of all things mechanical that we have come to accept and depend upon in this modern day and age, nothing can produce a pure and lasting hatred as can an outboard motor. If one's automobile dies on the highway, at least one can get out and walk away to find a telephone to summon help or whatever. But if your outboard breaks while you are out in the middle of some decent sized body of water you're usually stuck and unable to remove yourself from the immediate vicinity of the very thing that has caused you so much pain and agony. Such predicaments if repeated often enough can produce lasting impressions which may be brought to the surface years later with very little provocation. While a bad reputation can often be weathered by companies manufacturing other items, such feelings can spell instant trouble for an outboard maker. Although problems with Scott-Atwater's large thirty and thirty-three H.P. motors of 1955 and 1956 may not have been a deciding factor in the company being sold to McCulloch Corp. in 1956, they certainly didn't help.

Though there are many smaller Scott-Atwaters still in service today, these big engines of the mid-fifties all but disappeared within a few short years and when the previous incident occured in the late sixties they were almost non-existant. Not long ago a local dealer confided that he had purchased thirty of these big outboards in 1955. _____ I say big because Johnson and Evinrude's largest engine of that time was but twenty-five H.P. Anyhow, the dealer sold the first fifteen motors, but was forced to retain the second fifteen to provide parts to keep the others going. The dealer further stated that his association with Scott-Atwater terminated at that point. I don't really think things were all that bad, but they may have been close. These Scotts had their troubles, not the least of which was their frequent and maddening refusal to start. Scotts required a little extra care in their operation; something that a care-free boating public was generally unwilling to give. That critical balance between spark and fuel-air mix could easily be upset and render the outboard useless to the average boater. Even the Bail-a-matic, an exclusive Scott-Atwater feature that incorporated a separate pump system located in the upper tower housing of the outboard that would bail your boat at idle speed, would of course not work if the engine would not run.

Yet, of all outboard makers who have been absent from the scene for at least twenty-five years, the name of Scott-Atwater remains probably the most recognizable. Scott-Atwater first manufactured outboards under their own name in 1946, although they had manufactured outboards for Earle DuMonte since the mid thirties. Before World War II Champions were marketed through Firestone tire outlets, but in 1946 Scott-Atwater assumed the contract for these motors also and henceforth they were known as Firestones which were really Scott-Atwaters in disguise. Scott-Atwater was also responsible for the manufacture of other private brand motors such as Corsair, Mariner, and Hiawatha for brief peroids. DuMonte, however, formed a separate company to build his Champions and continued in business until 1957.

By 1950 Scott-Atwater was enjoying a marked success with its line of engines ranging from 3.6 to 7.5 H.P. and in that year entered the mid-range field with new ten and sixteen H.P. models. The engines pictured here are from that happier time in Scott's existence and deserve further mention. The outboard to the left is the 1951 model 519 which in addition is identified by the 1-30 on the side of its automatic rewind starter. The 1-30 indicates the speed range of this engine and under light load conditions the 16 H.P., 20 cubic inch outboard will come very close to 30 M.P.H. Scott used these figures on the side of all their models during this period. The 10 H.P. was 1-25, the 7.5 H.P. was 1-20, and so on down the line.

The model 519 is an alternate firing twin that develops its 16 horsepower at 4200 R.P.M. and has full forward, neutral, and reverse shift capabilites. Ball, roller, and double roller bearings were used throughout this quality built motor. Its fuel system utilized a single hose from the six gallon auxiliary tank with a fuel pump on the engine while O.M.C. and later Mercury chose to use the double hose pressure method. One drawback was the outboards weight which at 88 pounds was as much as 20 pounds over the competition, but then the 519 was a substantially built outboard. The price was $359.50.

The engine on the left is indeed a rare bird today, although at the time it was considered more of an odd duck. It is the racing version of the 20 cubic inch model 1-30 built in 1952. It was hoped the engine would compete in class "B", however it proved to be a disappointment. The weight of the powerplant was placed higher above the transom thus making it top heavy. Additionally, though a fine engine, the Mercury Hurricane was a better one____and faster. Therefore the Scott-Atwater Green Hornet, as it was called, never did make much of a name for itself.

There are a great many fifties outboards out there in outboardland gathering dust for the sake of some small needed part such as a water pump impeller. A substantial number of these are Scott-Atwaters. There are few quick-fix solutions to most of these problems, but with a little thought and ingenuity; who knows? After all, what do new outboards cost these days?

ANTIQUE CORNER
by
Lawrence Carpenter

The Evinrude Sportwin

Of the dozens of different models produced by Evinrude during its history, which now dates back some seventy-four years, perhaps no other model has enjoyed such continued popularity as has the Sportwin. If we discount the heavy iron and bronze single cylinder rowboat motors that were built by the company from 1909 to 1922, the Sportwin, when it was introduced in 1923, revolutionized the entire Evinrude line in a few short years.

During the teens, the rowboat or knucklebuster class of engine was being manufactured by the entire industry, with but a few companies straying from this design concept. Cumbersome though they were, these motors filled a need and were purchased by the tens of thousands. However, one of the faults of these outboards was the vibration they caused. Attempts at balancing these heavy singles was somewhat of an afterthought and the truth was that they could shake your teeth out. After World War I two new companies emerged to design outboards of the opposed two cylinder varity. This concept placed the cylinders at 180 degrees to each other on either side of the crankshaft. The cylinders fired at the same time, thus greatly reducing engine vibration. There had been a few opposed engined outboards of earlier vintage, but poor breathing characteristics had limited their popularity. These new outboards had the benefit of more refined engine building practices and were constructed using liberal amounts of aluminum, a metal which had come into its own during the war.

The first of these motors was the 1921 Elto Light Twin designed by Ole Evinrude who had sold the company bearing his name some years before and now sought to return to the outboard business. The second motor was the new Johnson twin, introduced late in 1921. During the 1922 season these two outboards swept the boating scene, catching the rest of the industry somewhat by surprise. Evinrude, not to be outdone, prepared to offer its own new outboard in the two to three horsepower range for 1923. Keep in mind that this was about as large as these engines had gotten at this time. The outboard was still a powerplant relegated to rowboats and canoes.

The new Sportwin offered features the competition did not. A new reversing lower unit operated by the tiller handle gave the Sportwin greater versatility at dockside. Later, a built-in generator provided power for an onboard light to assist fishermen after dark. Another nice feature was a transom clamp which locked with a key, thus helping to prevent theft. A saltwater model of the sportwin was also offered, its entire lower unit being built from bronze.

Production figures show that the Sportwin took third place behind the lighter Johnson and the more powerful Elto, however there were still plenty of eager buyers and this engine went a long way toward putting Evinrude back on its feet from a technological as well as a sales standpoint. 1927 saw the company add larger versions of this engine to its line in the form of the Fastwin and Speeditwin and Evinrude was ready once more to give serious challenge to the rest of the industry.

The Sportwin went through a period of gradual refinement during the thirties and early forties, and it continued to be a favorite of the weekend boater and ardent fisherman. After World War II it became apparent, however, that its basic design had run its course. The two Sportwins pictured here illustrate that point of change and the 1948 model on the right demonstrates a design which is not unlike modern outboards of today. The 1947 model on the left is the last of the opposed engined Sportwins. Though the specifications of these two engines do not differ greatly, the alternate firing principle of the new model made the operation of its predecessor seem rather clunky by comparison. Two firing impulses per revolution instead of one certainly made for a much smoother running motor. Other features for 1948 made the new model even more attractive. The tiller handle grip unscrewed to become a handy screwdriver for removing shrouds or making adjustments. A gas guage on the front of the tank gave instant notice of ones fuel supply. Other than its modern powerhead, Perhaps the new models most important advancement was its new "fisherman-drive" lower unit. Its angular drive gave a more efficient upward thrust direction for small non-planing boats and its truly weedless propeller insured fishermen greater freedom in those messy, weed choked places where the big ones lurked. Of special note to many was the fact that the slimmer, streamlined shape of this outboard took up less room in the trunk of the family car.

Although in later years the Sportwin lost its identity in Evinrudes myriad of model names ending in twin, the company built this same basic outboard for nearly two decades. Countless thousands are still in use and many an angler would prefer to give up his favorite fishing rod rather than part with his old Sportwin. Evinrude still builds small alternate firing twins, but the model name does not appear in present day listings. However, nostalgia is very big these days. Maybe the Sportwin will return.

Specifications

1947 Sportwin
Model 4371, Serial # 40033

Type	opposed twin
Bore & Stroke	1 3/4" by 1 3/8"
Cubic Inches	6.6
Horsepower	3.3 @ 3500 RPM
Weight	45 lbs.
Price	$ 122.50

1948 Sportwin
Model 4423, Serial # 02470

Type	alternate firing twin
Bore & Stroke	1 5/8" by 1 1/2"
Cubic Inches	6.2
Horsepower	3.3 @ 4000 RPM
Weight	39 lbs.
Price	$ 139.50

Antique Corner

The Evinrude Sportwin

ANTIQUE CORNER

by

Lawrence Carpenter

Penn Yan

In design excellence, superior quality, and vast model selection, very few wood boat builders were able to approach the standards set by the Penn Yan Boat Co. of Penn Yan, N.Y. from the mid twenties through the early sixties. Penn Yan built and sold every type of hull imaginable during this time from the smallest dinghy to inboard runabouts in the twenty foot range. Canoes, rowboats, sailers, hydroplanes, outboard runabouts, cartoppers, and yacht tenders also found their way all over the country upon leaving the New York facility. For those who at one time may have mused over this strange sounding name, its roots go back a great many years to a term one will seldom hear today. The term is Pennsylvania Yankee, a name sometimes given to grass-roots individuals of that section of the United States.

Although Penn Yan built a boat for nearly every purpose, their basic method of construction was somewhat more rigid in that almost all their wood hulls were of the cedar strip type or variations thereof. Indeed, long after most other makers had abandoned the cedar strip principle for more modern and time saving techniques, Penn Yan stuck with the proven cedar strip method. In its simplest form this construction consists of steam bent ribs of oak or cedar over which cedar plank strips are fastened, forming a smooth outer surface that can then be covered with a treated canvas and painted. The result is a light weight, strong, yet slightly flexible hull able to withstand severe punishment. Penn Yan perfected this method to a fine art during its years of wood boat manufacture and with the help of modern day materials, brought the cedar strip boat through the fifties and into the sixties. At one time during 1955 Penn Yan offered 167 different models. Monowood, Striplank, Composite, Triolite, and Plaston are but a few of the names Penn Yan created to describe variations on the cedar strip boat and many claim that no finer outboard hulls have ever been built. The key to their downfall was not found in any lack of quality or performance, but in the fact that they required regular and thoughtful upkeep and maintenance. American lifestyles seemed to be gaining such momentum that a great many people either would not or could not find time to do anything to their boats except use them.

As aluminum and fiberglass began to gain a substancial foothold in the industry, Penn Yan refused to give up its wood heritage altogether. The lapstrake construction method seemed to be about the last wood hull type still enjoying popular support during this period so Penn Yan entered this market in 1958 and in two or three years offered a complete line of these boats, both inboard and outboard models to over twenty feet in length. Dynamold was yet another Penn Yan name to describe a hull which combined an inner, less elaborate rib structure with molded plywood sections. It was born of a need to cut rising costs, but the Dynamold hull was near the end of the wood boat era.

Nearly everyone involved in the small boating scene excepting those very recent arrivals has a wooden Penn Yan lurking somewhere in their past. Though even the production of the lapstrake hull was phased out in 1966 in favor of a completely fiberglass lineup, the percentage of these boats is rather high in the total number of lapstrake hulls in existence today. Concidering the fact that builders such as Lyman and Thompson built many more lapstrake boats over a longer period of time, Penn Yan still makes a fine showing.

The Penn Yan shown here is from the rear of the 1956, 44 page catalog. It is the model CZT 12 foot Swift. The Swift model, built in lengths from 10 to 14 feet was the performance boat of the Penn Yan line and is fast becomming a favorite with those who are interested in the restoration of wood outboard hulls of the fifties. These graceful runabouts represent the epitome of Penn Yan wooden hull construction. The fact that they were very fast goes much father than their relatively light weight and can be attributed to a thoughtful and rather radical hull bottom design. The secret translated directly to a small wetted surface at speeds above 30 M.P.H. The vee of the hull grew slightly shaper toward the transom as it proceeded rearward from a point about two thirds of the way from the bow. This was just the opposite of most planeing hulls. The keel, of course, remained dead straight. At high speeds this design left the chines high and dry and the boat rode on only a very small piece of water, leaving practically no wake at all. Power was not wasted throwing water to the side and higher straightaway speeds were the result. Furthermore, the Swift lost none of its superb handling characteristics in its quest for speed. Its rounded chines would hold a high banked turn at full throttle without sliding or skipping and larger Swift models were highly regarded as skiboats. Penn Yan went into much detail to advise owners to properly set up and trim their outboards to take full advantage of the Swifts capabilities and even offered a transom height adjusting kit to assist along these lines.

Though the Swift is regaining some of its popularity today, a word of caution should be mentioned. This hull is a very intricate and complex unit and though there are still many surviving examples of this boat around, most are in need of a great deal more than a new finish. An amateur restorer should give a lot of thought to a project such as this and some professional help or advice would not be a bad idea. In my barn is a 12 foot Swift that most people would regard as just so much firewood. However, it is a Swift, it is saveable, and I never throw anything away. I've given the job a considerable amount of thought. Maybe next year.

Penn Yan Postscript:

As mentioned previously, Penn Yan, like most other boat builders who wanted to survive the nineteensixties turned to fiberglass as a means of construction material. And like most other builders over the past several years Penn Yan has felt the pinch of lagging sales, dwindling profits, and rising costs due to higher gas prices, high inflation, and the recent recession in that order. A news brief in the July issue of this magazine noted that Phil Bender, an avid boat enthusiast and corporate doctor, if you will, is guiding Penn Yan back into the mainstream of the small boat industry. Penn Yan, like so many other famous American brand names, deserves only the best of leadership in todays changing markets. Good luck to Phil Bender and Penn Yan.

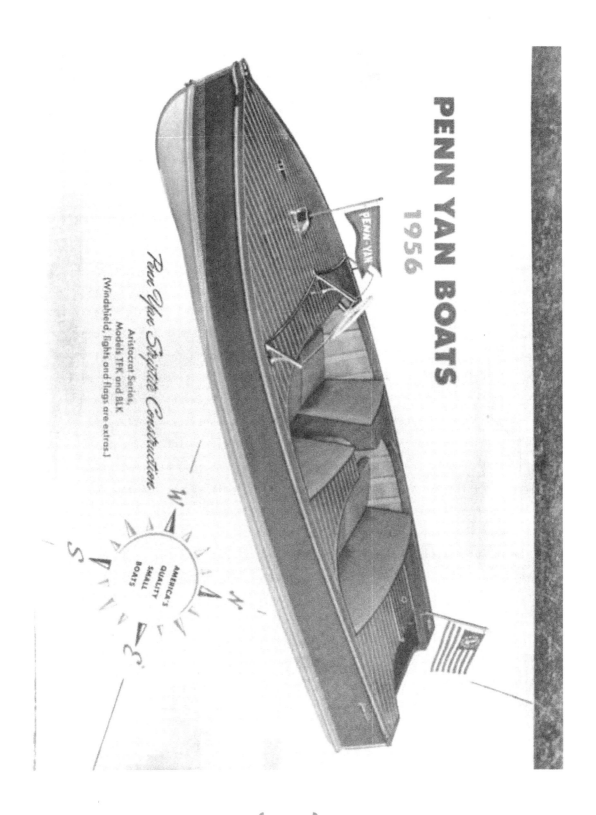

ANTIQUE CORNER

by

Lawrence Carpenter

1928 ELTO SPEEDSTER

The frequent reader of this column may have noticed that more outboards manufactured in the decade from 1920 to 1930 have been featured than those built during any other period. The reason is simply that the outboard motor saw more change and development in this relatively short space of time than any other. Although the outboard and the automobile share the same basic path of evolution through the first half of the twentieth century as the internal combustion engine grew from a noisy and unreliable object of curiosity into a smooth running, dependable source of power, automotive technology of the twenties was a time of steady forward progress. By comparison the outboard motor took a giant leap into the future. The year 1920 found the outboard, or "rowboat motor" an increasingly popular, yet a still primitive and cumbersome device able to accomplish little more than its name implied. By 1930 the outboard had been reborn to capture and excite the boating public as remote controlled, electric starting, four cylinder engines of 40 HP served to propell fast runabouts of considerable size or small cabin cruisers built to accomodate several people.

From the late nineteenth century until about 1910 gasoline and electric outboards struggled to convince the public that they should be taken seriously. Of the handful of American manufacturers that created the industry during this time, the majority lasted only a few years and of them all only Evinrude survives to this day. During the teens the outboard saw little change in basic design, however features such as variable pitch propellers, flywheel magnetos, and the automatic rewinding starter cord made their appearance. The first few years of the thirties were hard times for industry as a whole and outboard manufacturers were no exception; however by the middle of the decade makers began to put more emphasis on motors in the samll to mid-range category. During this period the smallest outboards ever made hit the market, the extreme being a tiny ½ HP model marketed by OMC. People were just beginning to regain their financial balance and many of these small to medium sized motors were more in tune with the family budget. The forties were hardly under way when the federal government placed a moratorium of the manufacture of outboards for public sale so that such companies might gear their production toward the war effort. By the close of the decade outboard makers were selling off the old and bringing in the new in an effort to compete in what promised to be the biggest market boom ever.

The fifites? Well, the fifties are interesting also because during this period the outboard got style, as did most everything else. But more importantly it became that which we would recognize as being not too distant a cousin from the product we might buy today. But the twenties? Ah yes, the twenties were the outboards golden age.

Few outboard motors of its day could equal the sound design and supreme quality exhibited by the Elto Outboard Motor Company's new offering for 1928, The Speedster.

Along with the Johnson brothers, the newly created Elto firm of Ole and Bess Evinrude had revolutionized the outboard motor with their new designs of the early twenties. When the Johnson's brought out their 6 HP Big Twin late in 1925 it was the largest engine to date and fully capable of lifting a small boat up out of the water and on a firm planing attitude. The race was on toward larger, more powerful outboards. Altho the Big Twin afforded Johnson a momentary lead over the rest of the industry, the new Elto Speedster and Quad models of 1928 put the company right back at the leading edge of outboard development.

The four cylinder Quad is a story by itself, so here we will take a closer look at the new Speedster. Ole Evinrude was not one to set his course based on the actions of others, thus when it came to outboard design the results may have seemed a curious mix of the old and the new to those concerned with contemporary trends. However the boating public was never disappointed with the product.

Like other Eltos, the Speedster utilized an Atwater-Kent battery ignition system when nearly every other manufacturer favored the magneto. Although Eltos carried their own coils, it was still necessary to supply an external 6 volt battery. Though this was an added inconvenience it was gladly borne because an Elto would usually start faster and easier than most other outboards which led to another feature associated with earlier motors. The Speedster, as did other models used a recessed, spring-loaded, pull-up knob atop the nickel-plated flywheel as the starting mechanism. Although certainly not of the dangerous, club swinging variety used on older knuckelbuster type outboards, its presence spoke of days gone by. But as I said, an Elto would start easily; a quarter-turn of the flywheel would do the trick and the procedure was as follows. (magneto equipped outboards usually required several revolutions of their rope cranked flywheels to start). After retarding the spark and setting a rich fuel mixture, one pressed the ignition stop button on the timer while rocking the flywheel back and forth against compression several times to prime or charge the cylinders with fuel. Then while releasing the stop button and bumping the flywheel counterclockwise against compression you let go of the knob as the engine started. Immediately you would advance the timer and as the motor warmed up, lean the fuel mixture, and you were off. By modifying this procedure the engine could be started in reverse or with a little practice either opposite direction could be obtained by manipulating the controls with the engine barely turning over.

The slim and streamlined lower unit on the Speedster was the most advanced of any outboard to date. The water inlet of the pressure flow cooling system is seen curving down behind the propeller which served as its pump.

The engine pictured here is an early 1928 model and was equipped with a cast aluminum gas tank as were the first Quads. These tanks were, however, difficult to manufacture and more than a few possesed a habit of seeping gasoline through casting pores. Subsequent engines were equipped with pressed aluminum tanks. The Speedster series, which began with this service model, continued for the next few years with several variations as Hi Speed Speedsters, Special Speedsters and Senior Speedsters joined the line. Major components of the Speedster group could be found on private brand outboards built by OMC as late as World War II.

Like other Eltos, the powerhead of the Speedster was ruggedly built and endowed with generous bearing area. It was difficult, if not impossible to wear out, if given decent care. Since receiving what was largely a cosmetic restoration several years ago this particular Speedster has seen countless hours of use and is eager for another generation or two of the same.

CARPENTER

SPECIFICATIONS

Engine Type	Opposed Twin
Bore & Stroke	2½" x 2"
Cubic Inches	19.6
Horsepower	7 @ 3600 RPM
Speed	25 MPH (using small light hulls)
Weight	62 lbs.
Cost	$165.00

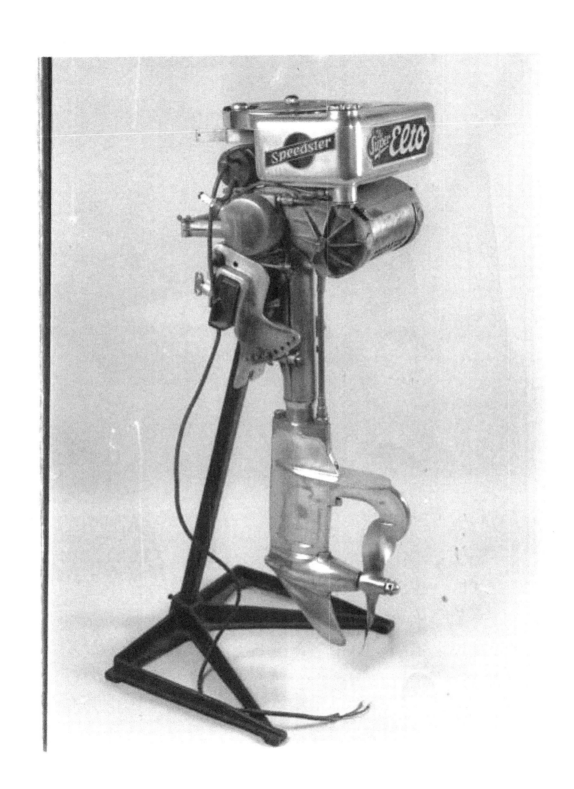

ANTIQUE CORNER

by

Lawrence C. Carpenter

A LOOK AT THE LONGSHAFT

Inboard engine installations are of course tailor-made to the hull that they power and the countless variations of the power application process are usually handled by the factory that markets a complete, ready-to-use boat.

The outboard motor is another story entirely. Due to its very nature of being a separately-applied, self-contained propulsion system, the outboard must be prepared to make itself at home almost anywhere and over the years manufacturers have succeeded in offering their customers a versatile product that would fill their needs.

Since the beginning, back near the turn of the century, perhaps the most basic question of adapting motor to boat has been how far the clamped location of the engine was to be from solid, pushable water, or more simply put; driveshaft length.

Early outboards were not too fussy and certainly not standardized, regarding shaft length. Displacement-type hulls were the order of the day and the props of these motors usually found themselves much deeper than necessary as the weight of outboard and occupants often loaded the average narrow-beam boat to a point that most would find unacceptable today. Many hulls of this period were not built with the outboard in mind and motors of this vintage were designed to be as adaptable as possible and with the help of a little jerry-rigging early outboarders could usually come up with a workable combination. Further, the basic tube-type tower housings and spliced coupling arrangement of the driveshaft assembly allowed a length adjustment of as much as several inches with many of these motors.

As outboard motors became recognized as something more than a curious oddity, their role in early powerboating was greatly expanded. Waterman, in the early teens, was amoung the first to offer factory-prepared outboards of a longer than standard length which the company stated as being 26 inches from top of transom to bottom of skeg. Any additional length to 35 inches could be ordered at no extra charge. If one required this measurement to approach 45 inches, seven dollars would do the trick. Longer still were models which sported special length transom clamps and a measurement of 55 inches from clamp hook to skeg. These outboards were clearly destined for commercial use or asked to perform auxillary power duties for large craft. The added cost went to twelve dollars.

During the twenties most manufacturers offered long shaft models and some makers would custom fit outboards to even longer shaft requirements. Johnson, who began production late in 1921, offered the longshaft almost from the first and the 1930's saw OMC expand their standard long-shaft line to include 15 inch longer models to compliment their shorter 5 inch extended outboards. To assist in the heavy tasks long models were usually asked to do, a rugged, lower ratio gear case was available which allowed the use of larger, slower turning propellers more able to push heavy loads.

As the planeing hull became the norm, standard length outboards were related to a transom height of about 15 inches. This distance was calculated to provide enough water over the prop to ensure efficient operation. Total distance from top of transom to centerline of prop shaft usually measured about 2 feet, but could be somewhat less.

During World War II the outboards were asked to perform anything but normal duty and shaft configurations were varied to the extreme as models utilizing several feet of extended length were built.

When the outboard went civilian once again in the late forties OMC, as industry leader, greeted the public with its customary complete array of motors. Mercury, on the other hand, as a newcomer to the field, chose to produce standard length models only, in an effort to concentrate directly on the center of the outboard motor market. This philosophy continued well into the fifties and therefore the Mercury Mark 20 pictured here is a rare variation of a common model. There were those at the time who decided that if Mercury would not offer the longshaft to the public they would build the necessary components to convert the standard Merc to the longer configuration. Several companies offered longshaft kits to dealer and customer alike, so most elongated Mercury motors seen during the fifties, as few in number as they were, were the creation of someone else. Mercury did not take kindly to these adaptations and at one point issued a service bulletin to its dealers warning against the installation of these kits saying that propeller thrust induced at this extended length might cause undue stress and dammage to motor support components not designed with this in mind. However I have never heard that these kits promoted any wide-spread failure of this nature, but as I say, longshaft Mercs were not a common sight. On behalf of Mercury it would be less than fair not to relate that when the firm did offer longshaft models a short time later, longer transom clamps and a beefier swivel assembly was included on these outboards.

In the nineteen-sixties when outboards grew in size and weight and the deep-V hull became popular, designers had to re-think and subsequently increase their ideas concerning standard transom height. The concentration of more weight on a deeply veed transom simply did not afford the necessary freeboard required and so as the purchase of extended 20 inch models in the larger motors increased, the 20 inch outboard became standard leaving the 15 inch as the shortshaft except on mid-range and smaller outboards, the further exception being the sailboat auxillaries. Now the 25 inch model is the longshaft.

If this short dissertation serves a further purpose other than relating the longshaft outboard it states that other than vastly increased horsepower and improved engine technology, there are few really new features offered today. As in many other subjects, if one digs a little they will find that we have all been down that road before and with outboards we may even have lost a thing or two along the way.

Remember those Scott Atwater's that would bail your boat? Now what ever happened to that?

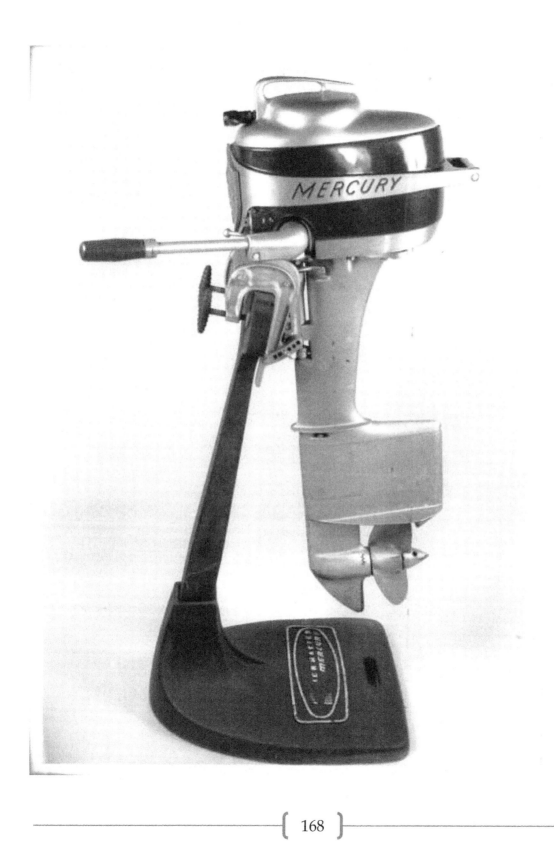

ANTIQUE CORNER

BY

Lawrence Carpenter

1957 Mercury Mark 75

The sound of tires in the driveway was followed closely by a few anxious barks from Willy, the doberman. W.W., a small brown terrier-type, joined in, an octave higher. W.W. came free with a tank of gas in Lawrence, Massachusetts one Sunday afternoon a few years ago when a regional gasoline shortage forced me off the turnpike in search of petrol. My wife and daughter could not resist that small wet nose pressed against the station window beneath the "free puppy" sign, so W.W. packed her rubber ball and food dish and came with us. The little dog soon displayed an amazing repertoire of facial expressions and an uncanny ability to jump six feet in the air, from a standstill, a feat which opened the eyes of friends and neighbors and was also responsible for W.W. breaking both front legs while still a puppy. W.W. now rules almost every other animal on the place, including a three-quarter Wolf Hybrid. W.W. loves boats and outboards, but enough of this.

I took one last look at the rare, old Tillotson pot-metal carburetor body distorted with countless age cracks, sighed a big sigh, and threw it in the garbage. I then closed my eyes tight a second or two, opened them, reached down and picked the carb out of the barrel and put it back on the workbench. Maybe I should see a psychiatrist, I thought and remembered to step back and glance out the shop window to verify that it was indeed my wife who had driven in the yard, back from her shopping trip down in Concord. It was, but then the dogs would have barked differently had it been someone else.

I looked up as Ann opened the shop door and smiled her "I know something you don't" smile.

"Come outside, I've got a present for you, or rather a couple presents."

The two outboards took up nearly all the available space in the eight foot bed of the Dodge pick-up.

"I stopped in at Haggett Marine while I was in Concord," was her explanation, still smiling. "And I guess they figured you ought to have these two."

Very kind of them I thought, but then the boys at Haggetts were very nice people.

The first of the two large outboards was a 1962 75 HP Elgin. Though basically a deglamorized McCulloch Flying Scott, this motor was not a common sight when new, as relatively fewer people chose to purchase an engine this large from Sears & Roebuck than did those who believed that future service prospects might be better at their local Johnson, Evinrude, or Mercury dealer. This particular engine looked quite decent, at least on the outside.

"They said the Elgin is locked up tight. A bad bearing or something." Ann added.

I thought I knew what the problem was. I had rebuilt a couple of the large three-cylinder Scott's and the trouble had centered around the lower cylinder which seemed to get hotter than the upper two. I had used an early sixty-horse model for a couple seasons a while back to the amazement of other outboard people who said it would never run properly. Admittedly, the design layout of these early three-cylinder jobs simply begged for a variety of irritating problems which presented themselves at the most inopportune times. However, after realizing that I could operate two cars and a truck on the gas consumed by those three big Carter model N carbs,

I had put the Scott on the rack with a few others of its kind. After a quick clean-up the Elgin would join the Scotts, frozen bearing and all.

Actually I had hardly glanced at the Elgin, my gaze quickly shifting to the 1957 Mercury Mark 75. Here was an engine I could really get interested in although I had never gone out of my way to acquire one for reasons I never fully pondered. I stepped over an array of controls and electrical harnesses with which both engines came equipped, to take a closer look.

"They said the Mercury was running fine when it came in about twelve years ago. Someone traded it in on a new Evinrude I guess. It's been sitting outside in back of their shop all this time."

Ann leaned over the side of the pickup and watched as I turned the Merc face up, grasped the starter cord and pulled it over. The engine was fairly stiff, but compression seemed quite good in all cylinders.

Few, if any outboard motors, ever arrived on the scene amid so much fanfare as did the first 1957 six-cylinder Mercs, nor had other new engines delivered the goods as did the Mark 75. Later sixes were larger, more powerful and performed with a quieter refinement, but that "Tall in the saddle" silhouette of those first motors created an impression of brute strength matched only by their performance.

Mark 75's were fast! As well they should have been, possessing 50 percent more horsepower than any other outboard on the market at the time. Even now, when discussing outboards of that era with someone else who has equally fond memories of these engines, the mention of the Mark 75 will frequently produce a nod and knowing smile.

"Those things were real animals", the guy may say.

Indeed the big Mark had an unabashed snarlyness about it and the heretofore unheard shriek of its two-cycle, six-cylinder powerhead held the unwary first-time listener in absolute awe. Furthermore, the then current crop of comparatively light-weight, shallow vee, or no-vee-at-all outboard hulls enhanced the new Marks reputation for speed and many boat-motor combinations conjured up by a devil-may-care boating public were little more than nautical time bombs that required only the slightest provocation in assuming an upside down attitude. Ralph Nader must have still been in school.

If the Mark 75 had a weak point it was to be found in its unusual method of acquiring reverse and to be fair it must be said that most problems here arose from improper usage rather than a bad design. The Mark 75 had no neutral and to obtain reverse one simply started the engine backwards. Thus the lower unit was a simple direct drive package.

Mercury as well as OMC were having problems at the time with the clutch assemblies of their full shifting lower units primarily because of an inability to garantee the limit of the engine RPM's while shifting. Mercury reasoned that the added torque of its new six would magnify these problems so the direct drive approach was used.

Operation of the "75" was handled through its new single lever control. "Puts 60 HP in the palm of your hand," said the ad. "Start engine with thumb button. Push lever forward for speed. Pull back for reverse. Easiest ever!---." Maybe so, but while many boaters were trying to re-educate their hand reflexes a great many boats got banged up during docking procedures, a fact not appreciated by their owners and of course blamed on the engine. It was simply the absence of a neutral gear that was worrisome and that deathly silence one experienced as the engine stopped while coasting swiftly toward the dock was more than many could accept. However, if the engine didn't start immedaitely in reverse the operator had a legal gripe. Additionally, internal safety limits on the new system sometimes failed prevent a nervous nellie from slamming the engine backward and forward repeatedly again and again causing lower unit damage. As a result of these misfortunes Mercury decided to go with a conventional type lower unit in a very short time. Sadly I have know of many Mark 75's that have probably found thier way to the scrap heap in later years because of an owners fruitless search for another lower unit.

The Mark 75 pictured here is not the one my wife brought home that day in our pickup. This photo was reproduced from factory material while my 75 rests on a heavy Merc stand of similar vintage in a room just off my shop. I have reconsidered checking the engine out my self in favor of handing the job over to Sam Baker, outboard mechanic par excellance and a vintage Mercury wizard here in the area. If, as I suspect, Sam says there is a lot of life left in the old Mark, a full cosmetic restoration will follow whereupon this fifties Mercury will ride again.

Last year I located a 14-foot Feathercraft aluminum runabout in very nice condition right down to its blue anodized hull andfifties tailfins. It is a ruggedly built, yet light weight example of vintage aluminum boat construction at its finest and though it comes very close to the off-the-wall type of rig I mentioned earlier, I just know the Feathercraft will make a fine home for this old outboard. The more I think about it the more impatient I get to press the button on this fifties time machine and allow the Mercury Mark 75 to vent its wrath on some of todays larger outboards. Whats more--- W.W. will love it!

Specifications

Engine type	in-line six-cylinder
Bore & Stroke	2-7/16" x 2-1/8"
Cubic Inches	59.4
Horsepower	60 @ 5400 RPM
Weight	168 lbs
Starting Method	Electric starter plus back-up auto rewind
Price	$925.00

1957

ANTIQUE CORNER

by

Lawrence Carpenter

HARDWARE & ACCESSORIES

A friend of mine has a variety of old marine items around his house. Some serve a useful purpose of sorts such as a polished brass deck cleat that now does duty as a paperweight and a jumbo-sized bow light that leers at you from a table in the corner with its converted 110 volt power. However, most are for display only. A very impressive mahogany steering wheel hanging on the wall, a solid bronze spark and throttle control, a binnacle, a prop or two, a bowplate, and back in the working set is a fog bell which signals any entrance through the front door.

Though this friend restores antique and classic boats for a living and so may well claim a special fondness for this water-borne memorabilia, the fact is that these items are showing up in the darndest places. People just seem to like these things, crafted in old world charm and constructed from substantial materials. They're just nice to have around and those who deal in these "nautical antiques" will tell you that traffic in this specific class of collectables is sufficient to warrant its very own price structure and desirability index.

During roughly the first third of this century, its starting point serving as an indefinite dawn of pleasure powerboating, many hulls purchased did not come equiped with supplementary accessories. Indeed a smaller outboard craft in anything but top-of-the-line dress had to be outfitted with the most basic of hardware by its new owner. This was a task expected by the prospective cuatomer who, though spending additional funds, could tailor his boat to his own special needs and tastes.

"I can do that now", I can hear you say. This is true, howevertoday you might be speaking in terms of electronic depth sounders, fancy radio equipment, hydraulic trim devices and the like. In years past the subject might well have been bow chocks, step pads, running lights or a steering wheel. Sure,you can still buy this stuff, but fewer people find it necessary.

After World War II the trend toward marketing a completely equiped hull really began to get underway and as competition brought forth fancier and more sophisticated craft, makers sought to provide many more items as standard equipment. The results were agreeable all around. Most customers wanted to jump in their boats and go and manufacturers increased profits by installing gear and furishings in increasing numbers.

Fiberglass almost completed the picture. Securing hardware in such locations as over an inclosed flotation chamber could present most owners with more problems than simply inserting a few screws into wood. Then to, fiberglass enabled builders to coordinate every last detail together in well executed style. Everyone was happy and most probably still are.

To be sure, marine supply houses continue to do a booming business, but few people realize how extensive selections were in powerboatings early days. Marine catalogs contained hundreds of pages listing thousands of fasinating items. Though Evinrude of the mid teens had hardly been around long enough to get its propellers wet, an Evinrude catalog had sixty odd pages and a large percentage illustrated a complete line of supplies, special tools, hardware, and motor and boat accessories. Additionally, several styles of Evinrude name brand boats and canoes were offered. The company certainly tried to cover all the bases as it sought to make a big splash in the new powerboating market.

Larger, more generalized marine catalogs offered the prospective buyer a staggering array of boating items. From bilge pumps and racing fins to diving boards and deck chairs, and on to canoe brackets and windshield brakets, or maybe a bronze eagle or possibly an electric power generating plant. One could outfit any boat from the smallest dinghy to the largest ocean going yacht. And for the latter, how about a saluting cannon? _____For yachts and club house use. Breech loading; takes ordinary 10 guage paper or brass shotgun "blank" shells. Has twelve inch tapered, rolled steel barrel, cylinder bored and with shell extractor. Mounted on a shapely cast iron carriage, supplied with heavy 3 5/8 inch wheels; all nicely japanned except for breech closure which is blued. Length overall, 17 inches; heigth 7 1/4 inches; width 7 inches. Barrel can be raised or lowered by elevating screw in carriage. Cost; $25.00 or $40.00 if chrome plated. _____It doesn't seem like it would have taken much to convert this trinket into a lethal weapon; possibly to ward off pirates?

A great number of marine antiques are selling for goodly sums these days, but only because the demand is there. In another forty years or so I dare say that such things as a shiny old bell or propeller will still be cherished. That new fishfinder you just bought shall have perished long ago.

L. Carpenter

Antique Corner

by

Lawrence Carpenter

Century Boats   1932

During the late twenties and early thirties pleasure boat technology was advancing at such a high rate that new developments were forthcoming on a monthly or even weekly basis. Not even The Great Depression could extinguish the boating public's desire to see what was just around the corner and manufacturers sought to gain a competitive edge that might translate into added sales which could keep a company solvent just a little longer.

The displacement hull was still very much alive, but lighter, more potent engines had powered the planeing hull and even hydroplane types to the forefront. Speed, speed and more speed was the order of the day and people just couldn't get enough of it.

In 1932 the Century Boat Company of Manistee, Michigan found itself under new ownership and those in command were determined to carve for themselves a larger piece of the small pleasure boat market. At that time the company was but a half a dozen years old. Production had always been limited and model selections few.

"Boating With The King of The Seas" was now the firm's lead line and a national advertising campaign signaled a new beginning. The photo seen here is of the folder listing the new inboard fleet and a run-down of these models is as follows:

Four sleek runabouts in lengths from 16 to 18½ feet comprised the Sea Maid series. Sea Maid models 46 and 47 were 16 and 17-foot straight inboard types featureing the new Gray Phantom 49 HP engine that provided speeds to 35 MPH with one person aboard. The varnished hulls were built of Phillipine mahogany and afforded seating for five passengers in their double cockpits. Prices were $895.00 and $985.00 respectively.

Sea Maid models 49 and 65 were 18½-footers with both cockpits located amidships. The Sea Maid 49 used the same Gray Phantom 49, however the model 65 sported the Phantom six-cylinder, 66 HP motor. Engines in these two larger Sea Maids were placed near the transom and were coupled to the tilting stern drive unit built by Johnson Motors. The result was an engine and drive system not unlike the modern inboard/outboard powertrain in wide use today.

However, these drive units were extremely heavy and together with a rear-mounted engine, placed a great deal of weight in the stern of a small runabout. Futhermore, they robbed much needed power from the engine and performance with standard inboard drives proved far superior as well as offering a better balanced boat. Customers and boat builders alike became quite willing to give up the advantages of the stern drive unit for these reasons and as Johnson Motors faced hard times during this period and the upcoming sale of the company to Outboard Motors Corp., the stern drive unit was discontinued. Though other manufacturers built similar units in the years thereafter, it would be many years before the I/O returned with a vengeance.

The largest runabout of the 1932 Century line was the Sea King 93. This sleek 22-footer featured a pointed torpedo stern design and its double cockpits afforded room for eight passengers. Power was from a 93 HP Gray Phantom and its drive train was of yet a third configuration used by Century; that being the Gray-built vee-drive unit. Like its smaller sister ships the Sea King came fully equipped with everything from Stewart Warner instruments to its Century designed self-bailer.

The price was $2,185.00.

Speed demon of the 1932 fleet was the Thunderbolt. Fourteen-feet in length, this inboard, single-step hydroplane was powered by a 125 cubic inch Gray racing engine which promised speeds to 45 MPH. The cost was $1,075.00.

At the bottom of the Century line-up, price wise, was the Pioneer and the Scout. These two 16-foot, sparcely appointed, open utility models were touted as boatings greatest value and became very popular as fishing and summer camp boats. The Pioneer came equipped with the Gray 32 HP engine and was priced at $497.50 The Scout utilized the 49 HP motor for $647.00 A good buy indeed, but keep in mind that 1932 dollars were difficult for most people to accumulate.

The Century boat line constituted a fine array of quality runabouts, pointed directly at the small inboard market, however every maker needed an edge or a plus over its competition and for Century this came in the form of what the company proudly introduced as its Air-Cushioned, Hydraulic-Action Boat Bottom. To describe this revolutionary new planeing surface it is best to refer to the company's own ad copy.

----The use of longitudinal steps, formed by overlapping planking, has been tried many times before, but has been thought previously to be impractical. It remained for Century engineers to discover that, by running the shoulder section or plank edges of these longitudinal steps at a slight angle to the keel or center line of the boat, several things were accomplished.

First, it became possible to steer and maneuver such a craft in a manner heretofore thought impossible.

Second, through the use of this design frictional resistance to passage through and over the water was reduced as speeds increased and air was induced throughout the full length of the boat bottom at several points, thereby decreasing the wetted surface materially and increasing the speeds per pound HP to a point heretofore undreamed of.

But, most important of all, from the runabout owners standpoint, is the fact that this type of construction forever takes away the "bugaboo" of hard pounding experienced in the usual vee-bottom construction at speed, imparting a new and entirely different riding action of surprising comfort to even the fastest of pleasure runabouts. One ride in Century's new outboard or inboard runabouts will convince any prospect that nothing else will do -------.

Though this ad copy is, after all, only ad copy, it remains for those few who remember and those fewer still who STILL possess these boats to judge just how good the Air-Cushion bottom really was. However, Century has always been an innovator of new ideas and perhaps this is one reason why the company is very much alive at the present time while other larger firms whose names echoed the mahogany runabout in more classic terms have long since faded from the scene. Although during the past 25 years the name Century has been associated primarily with its fine line-up of inboard hulls, there were periods throughout its earlier existence when Century outboard boats of both pleasure and racing varieties may well have been more responsible for keeping the company on a firm financial footing.

In 1980 the Century Boat Club was formed for those who own or simply have an interest in Century wood hulls which were built until 1969. Anyone seeking more information should send their request along with an SASE to Bob Speltz, 505 Albert Lea St., Albert Lea, MN 56007.

ANTIQUE CORNER

by

Lawrence Carpenter

1902 SUBMERGED ELECTRIC

The internal combustion engine had just made it into the pop-bang-boom stage and it arrived with a cranky disposition. It could whack you with its moving parts or shock you with an electrical charge. Even at rest, a state it often assumed with daring obstinance, it looked an odd and unfamiliar assembledge of parts.

But no matter how raucous and unreliable the gasoline engine was as it emerged from its cradle, it promised the magic of motive power more suitable to the needs of the individual than did those monstrous hissing steam engines. Inventors and gadgeteers by the thousands worked tirelessly as they applied the gas engine to a wide range of uses. The area of transportation was of course their favorite endeavor and it was said that wind power, pedal power, and old fashioned horse power would soon be anachronisms in a new and modern age. Indeed, powered flight was waiting for just such an engine to get off the ground.

The idea of removable, outboard mounted power for small boats had been around for some time and both here and abroad enthusiasts created the first gasoline outboard motors in crude, but workable configurations. However motors small enough to be utilized as outboards were still quite heavy considering the limited power they produced and so during these early years more serious attention was directed toward the inboard mounted boat engines.

There was, however, another power source just now coming into its own: Electricity. Actually the first outboard devices had used electric motors which transferred power to the propeller via a chain drive setup, and at the turn of the century the electric motor enjoyed certain advantages over its gasoline counterparts. It was simple, clean, quiet, and reliable, and though not having the power of a small gasoline engine, at this stage in the game it came quite close. Consequently we find that it was the electric motor that introduced the outboard concept to the boating public.

In 1900 the Submerged Electric Motor Co. was established in Menomonie, Wisconsin in a group of buildings formerly occupied by a lumber company. Though wrongly referred to as being America's first outboard motor factory, it was indeed a very early effort. Jim Webb in his book "The Pictorial History of Outboard Motors" reports that the firm was organized by Wisconsin Senator James Stout who was also the originator of the industrial arts program in our public school systems. The inventor of the Submerged Electric was one Tracy Hatch.

Although this early outboard appears indentical in concept to modern electrics, there is one startling difference. Water was not sealed from the motor by the case, but was actually allowed to have access to the engine itself, thus lubricating its moving parts! The salt water version of this motor did come equipped with a sealed case; however instructions stated that the case be filled with fresh water and the level of such be maintained slightly above that of the surrounding salt water.

A great deal was made of the fact that the motor steered the boat as well as propel it. Thrust direction and rudder were as one as the entire unit swiveled on its transom bracket like any outboard made today. Reverse was obtained by simply turning the unit 180 degrees.

The tubular stem or tower housing allowed for adjusting the depth of immersion or transom height. The battery cables exited from protective arms extending from either side of the upper ball containing the "controller" switch. These cables were further utilized as tiller lines.

Storage batteries, or rather accumulators as they were called, were housed in separate boxes of two cells each and were specially designed by the company for use with their motors. Two boxes provided standard power for the smaller of the three sizes of motors offered. Thus equipped the Submerged Electric could be expected to push a twelve to sixteen foot boat up to twenty miles at a speed of four to five miles per hour on a single charge.

Prices during the period of 1901-1902 ranged from $100.00 for the standard B-1 model to $150.00 for the largest B-3. Battery prices were $25.00 per box of two. The B-1 could handle three such boxes. Six could be used with the B-3.

The company touted its motors as adaptable for use on rowboats, fishing, hunting and pleasure boats of all kinds, launches, yacht tenders, as well as auxiliary power for sailing craft. Although production figures are not available this writer would estimate that several hundred to possibly a few thousand of these electric outboards may have been produced during the early 1900's.

The Submerged Electric today is not a common engine, but it is not among the most rare of antique outboard motors. Several are known to exist and I am sure that at least a few dozen more reside comfortably in attics and cellars where they have been for many years.

The B-1 model pictured here is in very good original condition. At some point in the future a cosmetic restoration will include nickel plating the entire unit except for the bronze transom clamp and the removable aluminum skeg or fin. Traces of plating indicate this is how the motor appeared when new.

About 1906 when gasoline powered outboards began to be noticed by more than a few people the Submerged Electric Company decided to market such an engine themselves. The result can best be described as a much older looking version of the Clarke Troller (Antique Corner - June 1982). The powerhead was submerged in true company fashion, but this time of course sealed in its protective underwater case. The introductory price was a more reasonable $75.00. Very little is known about the "Portable Gasoline Submerged Propeller" and I know of no examples that have surfaced to date. Anyone out there have one tucked away someplace?

It is doubtful that this later outboard met with much success, for as Waterman and then Evinrude began to market their motors in increasing numbers, no mention of the submerged engine is evident.

However, the Submerged Electic Motor Co., along with a very few other firms, had performed a valuable funciton. They had proved the concept of detachable outboard power for small boats and had shown that their products had a place in the industry. Simply put; they invented the outboard motor.

Same Place - Same Date
Evinrude's 75th Anniversary
&
The Antique Outboard Motor Club National Convention
by
Lawrence C. Carpenter

Lake Okauchee, Wisconsin was the place and the last weekend in July, the date, as members of the Antique Outboard Motor Club assembled friday morning at the Golden Mast Inn to run and display their finest old outboards.

This year's turnout promised to be the largest ever. Evinrude was sponsoring a portion of the meet as they in turn celebrated the 75th anniversary of their first production motors back in 1909. To complete the nostalgic setting for the event, this small southern Wisconsin lake was chosen because it was here that Ole Evinrude first conceived his outboard motor.

Although AOMC members arrived with outboards of many different brands, more Evinrudes than usual were present in honor of the occasion. The Evinrude Company, well aware of its rich heritage, has always supported the goals of Antique Outboard Motor Club for it is the only National and indeed worldwide body that actively restores and preserves this corner of boating history.

As the number of engine stands displaying beautfully restored outboards grew along the shorefront, many members launched their older hulls on which to run their motors. Several first model, 1909-12 Evinrudes were run as well as a wide selection of later, more powerful antiques.

Sam Vance of Unadilla, N.Y. ran his rare 1931 40 HP electric-starting Elto Big Quad.

Bob Grubb of Pottstown, Pa. had his 1951 Mercury Hurricane almost continually in action.

Bob Davis of Mountain Home, Arkansas displayed a flawless 1928 Elto Quad which eventually took the best overall restoration trophy at Saturday night's banquet and Bob's 1898 Submerged Electric outboard proved to be the oldest running engine at the meet.

A large display of early Evinrudes was set up by Dora Kawalek from Minneapolis.

Many vintage racing engines found their weay to this meet and several were clamped to the transoms of those old hydros and runabouts that vied for national championships way back when. The smell of racing fuel was enjoyed by everyone in attendance.

Saturday was Evinrude's day of festivities and by 10 AM, Ralph Evinrude himself had arrived to take part in the days events. Every antique outboarder was anxious to meet this fine man. After an elaborate noon-day picnic sponsored by the Evinrude Company and prepared by the staff at the Golden Mast Inn, a specially-built and custom trimmed 25 HP outboard was presented to Mr.Evinrude. This was the firm's 7 millionth engine and the manner in which it was received left little doubt that no other anniversary present would have been appreciated more.

The Governor of Wisconsin, Anthony Earl, had declared this day Ole Evinrude Day in recognition of Ole and his wife Bess, who were equally responsible in creating the outboard motor industry and to acknowledge the principles and ideals by which the companies of Evinrude, Elto and finally Outboard Motors Corp. flourished under their leadership. Their son, Ralph Evinrude, born to them in 1907 has actively pursued these same ideals and kept them at the forefront of company policy for over fifty years. As a result, Evinrude still retains a strong personal identity absent in so many other large corporations of today.

Later Mr. Evinrude took a personal interest in looking over the antique outboards much to AOMC members delight. The beautiful Elto Quad of Bob Davis' held a special meaning for him as it was this model, the first production four-cylinder outboard which Ralph Evinrude had been instrumental in developing during the mid to late twenties.

As saturday afternoon passed it came time to pack up and think about the long trip home. The banquet still lay ahead that evening, but everyone knew the hands-on fun of this years meet was at an end.

Many members, I'm sure were already thinking about next years National Convention. At Evinrude, however, next year is nearly here. Those production V-8's are on their way.

Double-header at Okauchee Lake, Wisconsin

The Antique Outboard Motor Club National Convention

&

Evinrude's 75th Diamond Jubilee Anniversary

by

Lawrence C. Carpenter

On July 27th through 29th this summer past, the mid-west chapter of the Antique Outboard Motor Club hosted the annual National Convention at Lake Okauchee, Wisconsin. A record number of members from all over the U.S. and Canada attended, for this year's meet bore special significance, a clue to which could be found in the location itself.

Long ago Ole Evinrude conceived the idea for his first outboard motor as he rowed furiously across this very lake carrying a supply of ice cream for his future wife Bess and a small group of friends. The mid-day sun did little for the ice cream, but the hard and monotonous labor of rowing left Ole's mind free and relaxed to envision his own motor-making genius applied to a device capable of powering a small boat. This event has been told and retold many times until now it lies deep in Wisconsin folklore, so it is of little wonder that the Evinrude Company, a firm that preserves and respects its heritage well, chose this location to celebrate the 75th anniversary of the marketing of those first few outboard motors back in 1909. The combination of the two events promised a dream weekend for AOMC members and many who had never attended a national meet were determined not to miss this one.

The Golden Mast Inn opened its beautiful grounds and shorefront as the site for these festivities. My wife Ann and I arrived shortly after 8:00 AM friday morning, an hour I had suspected might be a bit early, however we were greeted by the sight of a dozen or so members already unpacking a wide variety of prized restored outboards. Many also brought gleaming vintage outboard hulls on which to run their engines and it wasn't long before the morning air was split by the welcome sounds of aging iron.

The cooperation of many groups and individuals had to be secured before this event could take place and mid-west chapter president Robert Wagner and crew and Evinrude public relations personell directed by Jim Jost and Charlie Plueddeman had done a fine job over several months to insure that everything went smoothly.

Nearly perfect weather had been forecasted and by the middle of the morning a few lingering clouds had given way to bright sun and moderate temperatures. As engine displays began to take shape along the shore, I wrestled the three old Evinrudes we had brought from their nesting place in back of the pickup. Over the activities drifted the greetings of those seeing old friends and others one had previously known only by phone conversations or letters. Attentions wavered only to catch a glimpse of what treasures would emerge from the next vehicle to back down to the staging area. Whether it be antique outboards or any other hobby the pleasant bond between those actively involved in their favorite pasttime is not only immensely satisfying, but has the ability to make minutes seem like seconds.

By noon friday one of the finest group of antique outboards ever to be seen in one place had been assembled along the lawn of the Golden Mast Inn next to dockside. The ages of these motors reached back to the turn of the century and though a variety of makes, past and present is certain, if not silently required at any antique outboard meet, it was easy to note the heavy Evinrude population in honor of the occasion. Ralph Evinrude would be arriving on Saturday and everyone was anxious to meet this fine gentleman, son of the founder of an industry and one who himself had taken a leading role in guiding the fortunes of the outboard motor through good economic times and bad and one World War since the late twenties.

Leonard Pangburn of Minneapolis brought an impressive group of twenty restored outboards housed on their own custom-built display trailer. The companies of Waterman, Wright, Ferro, Lockwood, Caille, as well as Johnson and Evinrude were represented. The long racks supporting the outboards along each side of the trailer are hinged so that they may be winched in toward the center of the vehicle for safe travel.

John Scheurer from Mansfield, Ohio arrived with some of his favorite restored Mercurys of the older dark green and silver variety with the gleaming gold of a mid-fifties Mark 20-H nestled among them. John also had a nice Evinrude model A on hand.

Sam Vance of Unadilla, N.Y., also known to club members as Mr. Elto could be seen driving his 1931 40HP Elto Big Quad several times during the weekend. This rare Elto features an early Owens Dyneto electric starter and the engine performed as it did when new. Sam has also faithfully reproduced an exact copy of one of the original prototype Elto Quads as built by the company during the mid-twenties. This, the first four-cylinder outboard was built by mating an additional Elto Light Twin powerhead atop one of these early Eltos. This engine also ran well.

Bob Davis from Mountain Home, Arkansas arrived early and unloaded one of the finest 1928 Elto Quads ever seen anywhere. It might be well to mention here that Elto outboards were as much an Evinrude (name, not company) product as those engines labeled Evinrude for ELTO, whose letters stand for Evinrude Light Twin Outboard, was the second outboard company founded by Ole and Bess Evinrude in 1920. Bob also brought along his very rare 1913 German-built Hasse outboard, gorgeously constructed using large amounts of polished brass and bronze. The oldest running engine of the meet proved to be Bob's 1898 Submerged Electric. Bob Davis is not only a master restoration craftsman, but one of the club's ardent researchers and his work has uncovered many heretofore undiscovered facts concerning these old engines.

Dora Kawalek of Minneapolis and her family set up the largest display of Evinrudes from the companies early years of production.

Bob Brautigam from Bloomington, Minnesota and past president of the club came equipped with some of his best vintage racing engines complete with their matching hydroplanes.

Robert Grubb of Pottstown, Penn. ran a restored Mercury Hurricane on his fine looking 12-foot mahogany plywood runabout.

Bob Peterson brought his 1923 Evinrude model LAT, the only one of these rare engines to appear at the meet.

Lee Wanie appeared with a stunning post war Evinrude Speedifour as well as an excellent original 1955 Mercury Mark 55 featuring the unusual tiller handle steering, throttle, and shift control option.

Robert Lomerson displayed a fine military, extended shaft version of the Evinrude Lightfour.

This list could go on and on.

The noon-time lunch break came and went with hardly anyone noticing and it was time for some of the in-the-water events planned for the meet. The "Bang and Go Back" event requires a word of explanation. Boats with varying sized motors leave the starting point at full throttle. At the sound of the gun all boats turn and head for home. The first boat to reach the start-finish line wins. Speed during these runs is not important as the faster one travels, the farther they have to get home. One might think that everyone should arrive at the same time, however for various reasons this never happens. Boats are divided into two categories. Those above and those below 10 HP.

The predicted log race is a timed event in which boats run against the clock to complete their course in a predetermined time calculated by their drivers.

The entire cove where the meet took place is normally a restricted speed area. However local officials suspended these limits for the weekend to allow some of the faster boats to unwind a little. Local shorefronters were asked if they might relinquish the water to the antiques just this once and their cooperation was nearly complete as most enjoyed watching the show from their docks and many from the surrounding area came to get even a closer look.

Friday was fast coming to a close and members were busy securing their displays for that night. Local police from the town of Oconomowoc had been on hand all day to assist in traffic direction and parking and the Evinrude company had arranged for two off-duty officers to keep an eye on things through the night. The Golden Mast Inn is a very famous resturant in the area and as many as a thousand dinner patrons were expected that evening. The security for the displays was more to guard against a curious onlooker accidently disrupting a fragile old engine than anything else. Most club members were more than glad to leave their motors where they were than pack and unpack again the next morning.

The sale and trade of engines, pieces thereof, and reproduction parts is always a portion of any antique outboard meet and although a national meet is more geared to bringing out ones rarest and best, a certain amount of this activity was evident and welcome here. Several members hauled items halfway across the country to be picked up or exchanged at the meet.

More running and showing of antique motors filled Saturday morning with pure enjoyment. Bob Thornton, veteran race driver and engine builder from Castleton, Virginia slipped his class "F", Evinrude 4-60 powered hydro into the water and prepared for a speed run. Though Bob experienced a momentary sparkplug problem and had to pull the old engine over several times I think we all enjoyed watching him at work. His competent, practiced movements left no doubt in anyone's mind that here was experience in motion. When the 4-60 finally caught and held, the smell of racing fuel filled the air and Bob was a couple hundred yards away. Incurring the wrath of lake patrol officers as Bob strayed outside a buoy while trying to operate the racer in the confined area, the patrol boat took up pursuit, blue lights and siren ablaze. Bob returned to dockside in his own good time. The patrol boat idled off-shore to the boo's of the crowd and the officers decided not to press the issue.

Saturday had been designated as Evinrude's part of the weekend and everyone eagerly awaited the day's events which commenced with the noon picnic sponsored by the Evinrude Company and free to all registered AOMC members. The picnic, as prepared by the staff of the Golden Mast Inn, turned out to be a sumptuous feast, enjoyed by all.

Closely guarded under a shroud near the podium was a specially prepared, one-of-a-kind 25 HP Evinrude as a surprise presentation gift to Ralph Evinrude. This was the firm's 7 millionth outboard and the engine had been painted and trimmed to appear identical to the new 150 HP anniversary model which stood beside it.

A Proclamation was read from the Governor of Wisconsin, Anthony Earl, honoring the Evinrude family in announcing July 28, 1984 as Ole Evinrude Day in the state. Executives of the Evinrude Company spoke in turn and as they did the affection they felt for Mr. Evinrude was well evident. Indeed, several of them could be heard earlier in casual conversations relating stories of this man's personal charm and integrity. Unlike many large concerns that have been transformed, merged, reorganized, sterilized and generally kicked around in today's business world, there is still a sense of family at Evinrude.

At last Ralph Evinrude was introduced to a standing ovation. Mr. Evinrude approached the podium and greeted the crowd. Then he spoke softly of his family and their roots in Norway. He spoke of his father and mother Ole and Bess, and how they started the Evinrude company and the principles they had built it on. With humor and respect he related some lighter moments and then as he closed his remarks he thanked those in attendance for their presence and support.

Earlier, during the meal, a young couple dressed in their vintage garb, had departed from shore in a slender old rowboat powered by a "first model" Evinrude motor. "Ole and Bess" would bring back some ice cream from the other side of the lake for anyone who wanted some, it was promised. An so they had, it was now announced to another ovation.

A little later Ralph Evinrude appeared among the antique engine displays, eager to inspect every one and pass a remark or two with their owners. This was the high point of the meet for many members.

That evening the club banquet was held at the nearby Olympia Resort where AOMC president Dudly Davidson addressed the 150 people present. Following this the meet awards were presented. Many of us were already thinking of next year's National gathering and that special outboard we would restore and bring with us.

As for the men and women at Evinrude? They know and care about the outboards they build and about the people who use them. A tradition begun long ago is ready for tomorrow and beyond.

75 YEARS OF OUTBOARD HISTORY

BY LAWRENCE CARPENTER

PHOTOS BY RALPH POOLE

Evinrude's 75th anniversary celebration and the Antique Outboard Motor Club's National Meet combine to showcase some of our American boating heritage

A re-enactment of Ole's inspiration for the outboard motor.

Mercurys look absolutely modern in this setting

suitcase-model outboards.

TBM's Larry and Ann Carpenter; writer, photographer, collectors.

Ingeniously-designed trailer for transport and display.

power for a canoe? Why not!

A lavish buffet by the Golden Mast Inn.

OMC's, Ralph Lambrecht, with his 1937 Johnson and 14-foot Thompson.

A fine display of miniatures.

A beautifully-restored Marchetti kneel-down hydro.

Music was in tune with the affair.

Antique Corner

by

Lawrence Carpenter

1952 Mercury KH-7 Cruiser

It looked like the sky was going to fall in the next five minutes as I navigated the last couple hundred yards of the Weirs channel at a little more than the legal 6 mph. An almost total blackness had crept out of the northwest and it now engulfed the whole area save a little patch of blue to the south. Even the faint breeze had just died.

I cracked the throttle open a bit more and was contemplating my chances of making the public docks at Weirs Beach in a somewhat dry condition when I noticed the open 14-foot Starcraft pull up around my stern and settle down to my speed a scant five or six feet off my port side.

"That's an old one, isn't it?" the man said, smiling at me, then looking at my outboard.

This guy had on a Hawaaian shirt so bright it looked battery powered despite the gathering gloom.

A slender boy about twelve I presumed to be the man's son clad in a huge lifejacket sat in the next seat forward and made a big production out of waving to me like I was a quarter-mile away.

I lifted my right hand about a foot off my knee in return and smiled at him.

"Yes it is," I agreed. "Built in 1952."

"Look, it's got the gas tank on the motor just like the one on our sailboat," the son exclaimed. His father nodded.

"Run pretty good, does it? How many horse, about seven and a half?"

"Ten", I answered.

"Let's race!" the boy exclaimed.

We were nearing the headwaters of the channel as it opened into Lake Winnipesaukee.

The father chuckled apologetically for my benefit.

"That wouldn't be fair," he told his son. "We've got a brand new 25 here."

"But he's got a smaller boat", the boy argued.

As I was searching for the right words to unenthusically submit to such an activity the father said, "Maybe we could just turn it on a little up there at the last buoy. Greg, here, would get a kick out of it."

"Okay", I shrugged. "why don't you go ahead when you're ready and I'll see if this thing will stay together."

I could see the guy shifting his weight in anticipation and Greg had turned to face forward in his seat, at the same time lowering his torso so as to forego any unnecessary wind resistance.

I had to smile as I turned to look at the old Merc. It's a dirty job, but somebody's got to do it, I thought. The sky had gotten even blacker except for an occasional lightning strike a few miles to the north and I seem to recall those first few widely spaced rain drops coming down.

Suddenly the Starcraft took off at a good clip. I reached forward to grab a seat support of the aging 12-ft Lone Star Fisherman with my right hand, the Mercury Cruiser has terrific torque off the line.

The model KH-7 Cruiser was a transition outboard for Kiekhaefer Corp. Since the war, the company had established itself as a major outboard manufacturer. This reputation had been built on solid engineering, quality, and performance.

By 1950 Mercury had become the dominant force on the race course. Outboard racing had gained much of its old sparkle during the late forties, but alas, OMC had decided not to build any more racing engines and this left a lot of loyal race drivers with some seriously aging equipment. Though many old Johnsons and Evinrudes continued successfully around the circuit it was primarily because Mercury hadn't built an engine in that class yet. These winning ways translated into sales.

But by 1951, the company found its outboards severely lacking in some of the features modern outboarders wanted and the full shifting lower unit was the number one item on the list. This deficiency became even more glaring on the large motors capable of powering larger boats. Johnson and Evinrude's 25 HP big twins outsold Mercury's four cylinder model KG-9 by a wide margin for this reason.

Mercury chose its "B" class engine as the base for its first really modern outboard. Very soon the rest of the line-up would follow.

The KH-7 was the first Merc to feature full forward, neutral and reverse shifting capabilities. The twist grip throttle was also a first on this outboard. A totally redesigned drive train gave this engine its load lugging power as well as most of the speed of its immediate predecessor, thus making its 10 HP rating even more ludicrous. Its proud owners were delighted.

The only drawback the Cruiser may have had was the smallish gas tank still mounted on its powerhead. However, next year's new Mark 20 would correct this error in dramatic fashion and if I may be permitted to borrow a widely misused automotive term, the Mark 20 and to some extent the "A" sized Mark 15 qualify as classic fifties outboard motors if these designations are ever applied.

The KH-7 pictured here was totally restored by Robert Grubb of Pottstown, PA. Bob is a very active member of the Antique Outboard Motor Club as well as a Mercury dealer. He has done a superb job with this motor.

The KH-7 Cruiser along with the KG-7 Hurricane, the KG-4 Rocket, and the KG-9 Thunderbolt were at the forefront of those Mercs that spawned the

company's reputation for building fast outboards way back when. Bob's extensive mechanical restoration speaks for itself here in continuing this tradition.

The Mercury Cruiser was built for one model year only, so it is not a common engine today. But look out you modern 20's and 25's. Don't get in the way of this old Merc.

SPECIFICATIONS

Engine type	alternate firing twin
Bore & Stroke	2-7/16" x 2-1/8"
Cubic Inches	19.8
Horsepower	10+ depending on RPM
Weight	70 lbs.
Price	$400.00

ANTIQUE CORNER

by

LAWRENCE CARPENTER

THE CAILLE LIBERTY

The guy had stopped by early Sunday morning to announce that I was his last hope. While his pained expression indicated that he was dying of some incurable disease, it turned out that he was on a quest in search of a prop for his 7½ HP Firestone.

A few minutes later we were in my shop while I filed a couple burrs off a propeller I had just taken from a Scott-Atwater parts engine. He accepted the prop from my hand like it was some priceless treasure.

I was beginning to believe that all this guy's reactions were travelling at about warp five when he spied the Caille Liberty Twin hanging from the rafters over in a corner.

"My gosh! That's a strange-looking contraption," he exclaimed as he stepped backward like the old motor was emmitting some kind of invisible rays.

I rubbed my eyes and cleared my throat as I prepared to offer a treatise so eloquent and amazing as would leave him absolutely speechless. "Yes, that is a Caille Liberty Twin outboard motor built by the Caille Perfection Motor Company in 1925 Or 26. I'm not all that positive of the year," I said. "It sets on the transom at about the same angle as you see it hanging there," I added.

The guy turned to stare at me in utter disbelief, his eyes wide and his mouth open.

"No kidding," I heard myself say. I was going to have to hurry this along, I thought, or I would be hysterical very soon. Besides

Antique Corner

my wife had asked me to take out the garbage just before he had arrived. Actually, I reasoned that an explanation of this odd-looking outboard could be reduced to a couple dozen rather concise statements if one got right to the point.

The Caille company began outboard production in 1913. (Antique Corner, January 1982) A few years later Caille took its standard single cylinder outboard powerhead and mounted it on a straight driveshaft with the prop at the far end. This outboard pivoted at the transom clamp up or down or from side to side much like an oar with power at its tip. Caille called it the Liberty and billed it as a shallow water outboard.

"Drives a boat where 'er 'twill float" ---though the thickest weeds, over sunken obstructions and well up on shore when landing ---- without the slightest damage, said the ad. Caille marketed the Liberty right along side its standard outboard line. "The motor no other dares to follow", the company claimed and promptly offered $500 to any vertical type motor that could follow the newly introduced Liberty Twin for 1924.

Surprisingly Caille did not seem satisfied with simply pointing out the advantages of the Liberty, but really knocked the standard vertical outboard. Surprisingly because Caille built more standard types than Liberties and this ratio would soon widen further with the introduction of larger motors.

However, sales of the Liberty did quite well in may parts of the country where mile upon mile of shallow water could be found in low lying areas. Under these conditions the Caille Liberty may well have been the only answer.

Caille was quick to utilize the statements of satisfied users

Antique Corner

to tout the special capabilities of these unorthodox outboards. One published endorsement read as follows: "I must have a Caille Liberty! They get away from me by driving their boats into shallows and weeds where I can't follow with my (blank) twin vertical type motor." ----- Statement made by a Game Warden ---name on request. Apparently in this case the poachers had the Liberty, the game warden did not.

The basic advantages of the Liberty direct drive principle was simply explained. ---"the drive shaft extends straight out from the stern of the boat and the motor is pivoted and so perfectly balanced that the slightest contact with hidden obstructions causes it to rise and pass over. The propeller of the vertical so-called 'tilting-type' motor receives a sixty-pound blow before it will tilt, for sixty pounds of pressure is constantly exerted against the boat's stern when in operation. When the motor does tilt its propulsion value is lost. When the Liberty rises over obstructions its propulsion value is not diminished. Furthermore it has no bevel gears to wear, give trouble, and require packing in grease."

The Liberty Twin was equipped with the latest technical features as well. The newest type Bosch magneto provided a reliable spark while a Zenith carburetor automatically metered the correct amount of fuel. A motorcycle style twist grip control on the tiller handle regulated the speed of the Liberty Twin.

To aid in the transport of the Liberty one could quickly disconnect the driveshaft and propeller assembly from the powerhead and place both units in the handy chest the motor originally came in. Caille further stated that packaged in this manner the motor could be shipped anywhere or carried on the running board of a car.

Production of the Caille Liberty continued for many years. The

Antique Corner

single was produced from about 1917 until the early thirties or shortly before the company ceased all manufacture of outboards. The twin had a shorter life span. It was introduced in 1924 and was available through 1928 and quite possibly could have been purchased for a year or two beyond that.

Caille was not the first to market such an outboard, nor were they the last. Some of the very first outboard types built during the late 1800's, both gas and electric, were constructed in such a manner. Today perhaps the greatest concentration of motors of this variety can be found in the Far East where many are home-built or backyard creations possessing a wide range of powerplants. I seem to recall James Bond himself racing down some inner city waterway in that part of the world wreaking his typical havoc in living color while using one of these rigs.

My guest that Sunday morning was so enthralled with the preceeding disertation that he wanted to buy my Liberty Twin on the spot and upon finding it unavailable, vowed to locate another like it that was. Indeed, so great was his enthusiasm that I became caught up in his mood to the point where I could have sold a dozen such motors had this many people presented themselves at my door.

As the guy left I had to remind him to take his Firestone prop.

SPECIFICATIONS

Engine type	opposed twin
Bore & Stroke	2" x 2"
Cubic Inches	12.57
Horsepower	2-3/4 @ 1200 RPM
Weight	48 lbs.
Cost (1924)	$140.00

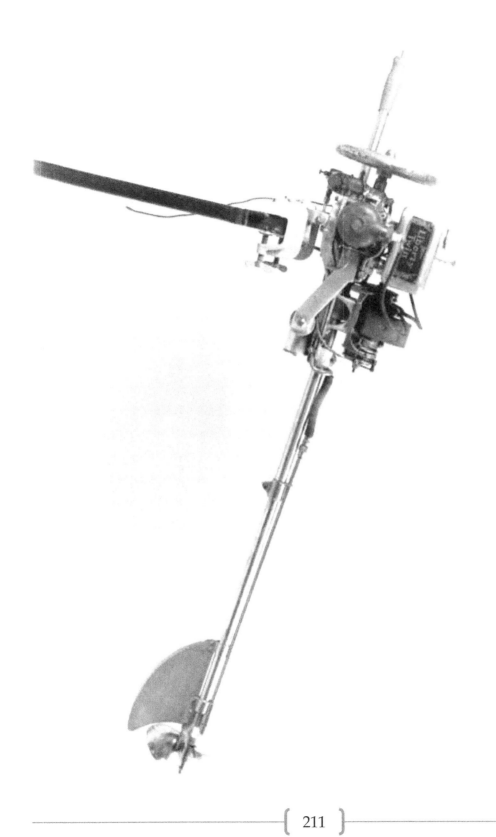

ANTIQUE CORNER

by

Lawrence C. Carpenter

The Dunphy Boat Company

Even today the name Dunphy remains one of the most recognized in the field of outboard-powered wood hulls, though the company closed its doors in the early 1960's as it refused to enter the age of fiberglass. There are still many of us who remember the quality and beauty of these craft and yes, there exists more than a few of these boats to rejuvenate this image lest we tend to forget.

The history of the company reaches back to the mid 1800's. Wisconsin, as well as the whole upper midwest was perhaps the small boat building center of the country and by the early part of this century Dunphy was producing a whole range of craft that included rowboats, canoes, duckboats, inboards of both commercial and pleasure types, and sailboats. As the outboard motor began to gain favor Dunphy courted this popular power source and along with other companies, both new and old, marketed a variety of these hulls until outboard boats comprised the lion's share of their production.

The catalog cover pictured here brings us to the period just before World War II. The Dunphy company had been heavily involved in military production during the first World War and to a somewhat lesser degree would be involved in this second such conflict. The company did not print additional catalogs during the war, though civilian boat production continued as best it could. However, Dunphy did release updated price lists throughout the war that related to the last issued catalogs. A special notice at the top of the sheet read as follows: Important! The specifications of materials for all Dunphy boats shown in the accompanying catalog (pre-war) are standard and will be adhered to as far as possible. The Dunphy Boat Corporation, however, reserves the right during the present war emergency to change specifications and make substitutions whenever it is expedient or impossible to procure materials specified.

While we're at it let's take a quick look at the boats offered in this catalog. To begin with all Dunphy hulls were of cedar strip construction, that is, narrow cedar strips fastened around tightly spaced oak ribs. Overall configuration was rather typical for this type of boat. What the company referred to as an "easy bilge" might be better expressed as a round chine though this latter term is technically incorrect. A Dunphy hull would lay up on its side and really lean into a corner, a bit of fun seemingly lost on most present day styles.

Oak half-ribs were placed between their standard counterparts throughout the running bottom. All fastenings were of copper and brass and all hardware was bronze. The outboard hulls featured mahogany finished decks. Special Dunphy Bakelite marine enamel in the company's own Sea Foam Green color adorned hull sides above the full length spray rails except for the top of the line runabouts that were mahogany finished. Most hull bottoms were all done in water resisting copper bottom paint.

Model line-up went as follows: The Blue Gill and the Tarpon were the basic fishing and sport-about hulls. Generally open except for short fordecks, the Blue Gill was slightly longer than the Tarpons. Lengths were from 12 to 16 feet and a rather tight price range went from $115.00 to $145.00. Highest recommended horsepower was 20.

Next up the model ladder, was the Dolphin and the Marlin available as fourteen or sixteen footers. The Dolphin was billed as an all-purpose utility boat, again with a short fordeck, but more staunchly built than the Blue Gill or Tarpon. Fordeck on the standard Marlin was much longer, however the deluxe model was pure runabout with a still longer fordeck, full center deck, and mahogany sides. Price for the 14-ft. Dolphin was $130.00. The deluxe 16-ft. Marlin went for $215.00. Horsepower rating for these boats was unlimited which in Dunphy's terms translated to the 33 HP Evinrude and Elto four cylinder motors of the day. Higher horsepower outboards of the early thirties were somehow forgotten or had all but faded from the scene. Evinrude's 50 HP Big Four would not be available until after the war and the 60 HP OMC 4-60 racing engne was not applicable to these boats.

The Sand Dab model, though available only as a 14-footer, had slightly more beam, a flaring bow and extra wide transom. The deluxe version with center and foredeck and rear seat back sold for $215.00. The Muskie was actually the 16-ft model of the Sand Dab. Deluxe price went to $250.00

Dunphy's fanciest and largest runabout was the Aqua Flyer. The 16-ft model with her 60" beam was priced at $325.00. Horsepower was unlimited, of course.

Moving on to other Dunphy hull types, we find the Sturgeon and the Northern Pike. These were gracefully styled rowboats, the latter said to be the world's easiest rowing rowboat. Outboards could be attached, but only up to 5 HP. The hulls in the 13 to 15-ft range were not designed to plane. Prices were $85 to $105.00

The Power Dink was another non-planing open type hull, this one equipped with a choice of two small air-cooled Wisconsin inboard engines of 3 and 4.2 HP featuring a built-in clutch and reverse gear. The Power Dink came in lengths of 14 and 16 feet and was said to be ideal for summer resorts, general sightseeing and utility use.

Lightweight of the Dunphy line was the Portage. Built only as a 12-footer, the Portage could be had in two models. The first was of extremely light canoe type construction, canvas covered to escape the drying up =and leaking process generally accepted as inevitable in cedar strip boats that might be in the water one day and out of it the next. The second model was without the canvas, but of heavier wood construction and could be dragged over shallow areas, marshlands, snags, or rocky beaches without damage, it was said. Weights of these car-top boats was 95 and 125 pounds respectively with prices of $105 and $100. The Portage was finished in Dunphy Forest Green outside with a natural finish inside. Maximum outboard horsepower was five with which this boat would turn on the proverbial dime while on plane.

At this time Dunphy was still producing a variety of completely-equipped sailboats up to 19-feet in length, but this line was dropped after the war. In 1946 the company introduced its first molded plywood hull and as this type of construction offered by many companies became increasingly popular the wooden boat reached its zenith and is a story for another time.

Like other wood boat builders, Dunphy switched to lap strake construction a year or two before the company's demise in the early sixties. Though not intended to be presented as a lower grade hull type, the lapstrake method allowed Dunphy and others to stay in business a little longer in a changing market. We can fondly recall an old Lyman or Thompson in their traditional lapstrake form, but hardly a Dunphy.

As I mentioned before, there are still a fair amount of these older hulls around to see, but sadly most of these are in need of some serious attention and every year more and more slip past the point of no return.

I'm sure you have heard of these drives or crusades which begin with the line "take a so-and-so or a such-and-such to lunch". Well, the heck with all that! Do something really useful. Save and old Dunphy!!

ANTIQUE CORNER

by

Lawrence C. Carpenter

OUTBOARD SALES LITERATURE

The 1985 outboard catalogs have been available in dealer showrooms for some time. Free for the taking, these "magazines" have reached an all time high in product illustration. Forty plus pages of brilliant color photographs, computer enhanced graphics and masterfully constructed eloquence combine to produce a dreamworld of ownership in the minds of those who open an outboard catalog.

But then nothing much has really changed. The state of advertizing art has advanced to be sure, but sheer effort and attention to detail have always been in evidence when promoting the outboard motor.

The cross-section of outboard literature pictured here reaches back to 1907 with an early Waterman catalog, but for our purposes lets take a closer look at the one in the middle. The Evinrude division of O.M.C. celebrated its 75th anniversary just last year. Fifty-one years ago the company's Silver Anniversary was commemorated with no less enthusiasm.

1934 was a year of mixed emotions for Outboard Motors Corporation. At that time flying the banners of both Elto and Evinrude outboards, the company had successfully climbed from the depths of the Great Depression under the skillful management of Ole and Bess Evinrude. But sadly Bess had passed away in the spring of 1933 and then little more than a year later Ole would follow.

However, by the fall of 1933 a completely re-engineered line of outboard motors was ready for public view and the cover of the new catalog, done in silver, navy blue, and white, proclaimed "Hooded Power" to be the wave of the future in outboards. Two new models were chosen to demonstrate this revolutionary new design achievement of a fully enclosed powerhead and truly perfected rewind starter. Indeed the only moving part not enclosed and shielded was the propeller.

Many other new features were incorporated into the entire Elto-Evinrude line. The genuinely modern outboard, much as we know it today, was born in 1934.

The interior of the 1934 catalog was done in black and white, however the execution of photos and illustrations was accomplished every bit as skillfully as with the 1985 edition. Furthermore, without counting every word I think its safe to say that this old publication has substantially more text in its 26 pages than the current one.

The inside front cover depicts the first 1909 prototype as the company's starting point and lists this engine's specifications. Page one contains an artists portrait of Ole Evinrude and a signed statement by him introducing the 1934 outboards. Pages 2 and 3 feature the new fully shrouded Lightwin and Lightfour models of 5.5 and 9.2 HP respectively.

The next four pages tout the new features of these and the remaining outboards for 1934. Paragraph headings read as follows: The New Lithtwin Imperial Fires Like a Four; A New Small Four With the Smoothness of an Eight; Only Three Simple Controls Project from the Hood; New Smoothness Attained by Rubber Floated

Power;Patented Co-Pilot Steers Your Boat When You Let Go; Simplex Starter Gives Starting Ease---Encloses Flywheel; Improved Flash Start Primer; Carburetor Silencer, Strainer; Spiral Bevel Gears, Underwater Silencing, Other Features; Propeller Struck Scores of Times -- Sheared No Pins; Built-In Rotary Valve is Gearless and Wear Proof; Four Motors Have Powerful 12-Volt Electric Starting; Eltos Have Battery Ignition-Evinrudes Magneto Ignition; Photos and illustrations accompany this text.

By 1934 the only difference between the Elto and Evinrude line was this method of ignition and the name on the engine. In the remaining years before WWII the Elto outboard would become an economy line of motors having less frills than an Evinrude and limited to small and medium range engines. After the War the Elto would not re-emerge save for one brief two-model appearance in 1949.

The next 8 pages of the catalog highlight the remaining outboards offered that year. Each page features one engine. Photos of the outboard itself and another of the motor in use are included.

The 2.2 HP Single was also built in full salt water dress utilizing all bronze components below the transom clamp.

The 4 HP Fisherman was the smallest twin for that year.

The 5.1 HP Lightwin weighed only 38 pounds and possessed a quick take-down feature that reduced this outboard to an 11" x 13" x 22" bundle that could be handled easily when traveling by train or motor car.

The 8.5 HP Fleetwin was claimed to plane raceaboats at 22 MPH and light hydroplanes at close to 30. This outboard could be ordered with OMC's combination electric-starter-generator, one of the smallest motors ever to be so offered.

The 16.2 HP Sportfour was the breaking point between medium and large range motors.

The Speeditwin was rated at 21.1 HP and was the largest twin cylinder entine in the line-up.

The largest service motor available from any maker in 1934 was the Speediquad. With 50 Cubic Inches and 31.2 HP this engine would propel a sport racing craft at over 40 MPH with two people aboard. These last three motors were available with electric starting of course.

The final motor listed was the all-electric. This outboard was not of the same configuration one is used to seeing today. It was simply the domed, circular, electric starting unit used on the larger motors placed atop a small transom clamp and standard drive-shaft and lower unit. The word that best describes its appearance is cute.

The following page delves back into the subject of special features; more details on some of the same listed previously and a couple they apparently forgot. Adjustable Driving Depth; Quick Take-down (Fisherman); Full Reversing, Flash Start Primer, Compression Release (other models).

A paragraph atop the next page explains that all horsepower ratings are certified by the National Outboard Association and are arrived at through sophisticated testing procedures conducted by the famous Pittsburgh Testing Laboratory, namely the electric dynamometer. The rest of the page attempts to answer the printed question "Which Motor Is Best Suited To My Boat?" A handy chart containing the required information is illustrated below.

The next two pages contain very detailed specifications of all models that would rival the same section of any new outboard catalog. One exception, though, a small column to the right is headed "Additional Features" Yes indeed, someone thought of a few more.

Automatic Tilt-Up, Adjustable Stern Bracket, Remote Control,

Vibrationless Steering, and Extra Length Models.

Next we come to a catalog section that is missing from most current such publications but always used to be a standard feature reaching back to the very beginning. This was the personally signed outboard testimonial. Eighteen or Twenty such letters lauding OMC motors appear in print from various sections of the country. Also appearing here are several photos with one-word titles that picture every conceivable use of an outboard; cruising, fishing, racing, aquaplaning, etc. One photo even shows three vacationeers in and around a boat, motor, and a rather rickety old dock. This title is "Cottaging".

Moving on we find two pages featuring the OMC racing outboards. The smallest is the tiny 7.5 cubic inch class "M" motor. Next we see the class "C" racing Speeditwin. Its 30 cu. in. displacement develops 30.6 HP at 6000 rpm and is capable of over 54 MPH on hydroplanes. Finally we arrive at the mighty class "F", 4-cylinder 4-60. This world record holding outboard is rated at 59.3 HP at 5500 RPM from 60 cubic inches. Top speed is over 60 MPH.

Further on we find that time payments, accessories, and warranties are discussed and additonal pamphlets, catalogs, and information are available on demand.

The enclosed price list is quite detailed. Prices range from $72.50 for the electric outboard to $385.00 for the Speediquad equipped with electric starter. The reverse side of the price schedule lists all Elto-Evinrude distributors (not dealers) in the U.S. and Canada.

The inside of the rear cover desplays a photo of the OMC factory in Milwaukee. One final paragraph reads as follows: Other Products of Outboard Motors Corporation include Lawn-Boy Power Mower, Hedge-Boy Electric Trimmer, Shop-King Combinatton Workshop, Speedibike Bicycle,

Motor, Portable Centrifugal Drainage Pumps, Portable High Pressure Fire Fighting Pumpers, Aquaplanes and Boating Accessories. Booklets and folders illustrate and describe each of these products. Ask for them. They are free.

On the back cover of the catalog appears the Winged Outboard Motors Corporation trademark.

Old outboard catalogs make for fascinating reading for anyone interested in the subject. Though avidly collected by some enthusiasts, they are overlooked by others. Although not on a par value-wise with automotive, motorcycle or even boat literature which is sought by many more people, this outboard stuff is certainly not without worth. Possibly the old marina in town has some old material up in their attic. Or just maybe it went out with the trash last week. It wouldn't be the first time I've heard that statement and I'm sure it won't be the last. To me its well worth saving for if nothing else those cold winter times when reading is the closest thing to doing.

ANTIQUE CORNER

by

LAWRENCE CARPENTER

1953 Mercury Mark 15

Shortly before World War II E. Carl Kiehaefer decided to get serious about the outboard motor. Five models in two basic sizes were offered for 1940.

Other makers were marketing extensive lines of motors and while many smaller engines had been modernized into trim, lightweight packages, some larger models still exhibited a bulky, clunky character inherited a decade before.

On the other hand, the new Mercury brand made its debut as a fresh face at a time when most Americans had improved their economic outlook and the boating public welcomed the appearence of these new outboards. The largest Merc of the day was but an eleven cubic inch alternate firing twin rated at six HP. However, in the deluxe version it weighed only 43 pounds and was very powerful for its size.

After the war this outboard, then known as the Rocket, reappeared along with the smaller Comet, a single cylinger model. In 1947 Mercury moved forward to meet the post war buying boom and redesigned its outboards. Horsepower ratings of the Comet and Rocket were raised to 3.6 and 7.5 respectively and above these two models appeared the Lightning, a twenty cubic inch outboard conservatively rated at 10 HP. It was not by mere chance that the displacement of this particular engine fell just below the class "B" racing limit. Soon the Lightning and its later easier breathing cousin, the Hurricane would set the cornerstone of the company's dominance on the race course.

1947 also marked the beginning of the famous Mercury green. Indeed, even today most boaters of middle age and older can recall a green merc somewhere in their background. As Mercury acquired a reputation for precision built, fast outboards, the eleven inch Rocket continued to be built until 1953 when with little change it became known as the Mark 7 to bring it in line with the company's new Mark series.

The Rocket remained a favorite with those who wanted an outboard of this size, but as Mercury sought to enter more racing classes the company took a careful look at the possibilities. The forty cubic inch Thunderbolt introduced in 1949 would be the class "D" entry and the little Super 5 of the same year would serve nicely in the tiny "JU" class. Class "C" would take a little more doing. This thirty inch class was still populated by pre-war Johnson PR's and Evinrude Speeditwins. Though somewhat outdated, these engines had received considerable attention from their owners and neither the drivers nor their outboards promised to fade into the sunset anytime soon. Further, a completely new engine of this size would take capital that Mercury could not afford at the time. Thus class "C" would have to wait a while as it did until 1956 with the introduction of the Mark 30.

But class "A" was another story entirely. Sadly the little eleven inch Rocket powerhead could not be stretched to approach the 15 cubic inch limit. Its size hadn't been based on class outboard racing back in 1940. As the engine used the same rods and pistons as the small 5.5 inch Comet single, the Rocket's displacement was simply twice that figure. However, downsizing the potent class "B" Hurricane engine was a distinct possibility and one that would not require nearly as much expensive tooling. Enter the 14.89 cubic inch model KG-4 Rocket Hurricane. In 1950 the current "A" engines such as the Johnson KR almost begged for a long overdue retirement and Mercury was only too glad to help them along with the Rocket Hurricane. As with its larger outboards of that period, Mercury rated this new engine very conservatively, even in stock form. Its horsepower was listed as being identical to the eleven inch Rocket at 7½ although the company did concede to add a plus sign after this figure on some listings.

Over the next couple of years Mercury reveled in its racing success to the point that the company may have neglected its stock outboards. The competition was offering features such as full shifting lower units and twist grip throttles that Mercury did not. As related in the Nov. 1984 column, the model KH-7 was the first Mercury to incorporate these features in 1952. The trend continued the following year as the company sought a larger percentage of the stock outboard market.

The two new offerings for 1953 were the first of the famous Mark series, the Mark 20 and the smaller, though almost identically appearing, Mark 15. Powerplants for these new outboards were the tried and true 19.8 cubic inch KG-7 Hurricane and the 14.89 KG-4 Rocket Hurricane (or Baby Hurricane as it was called) engines. But there the similarity stopped.

"The Shape of Things to Come is Here. Mercury slashes dead weight and dead bulk to give you most performance per pound of weight" said one ad. Mercury removed the gas tanks from atop the engine and introduced their pressurized six gallon remote fuel system. Beautifully styled cast aluminum shrouds now encompassed a super slim powerhead. Even by today's standards these outboards were exceedingly small in size for the power they produced. Horsepower for these new models was rated a little more realistically at 16 HP for the Mark 20 (previously 10 for the KG-7) and 10 for the Mark 15 (previoulsy 7½ for the KG-4). Engine RPM's at these ratings were 4000 for both engines, still conservative. Indeed RPM's for the previous models were never published, for had they been they would have appeared riduculously low to coincide with such small horsepower ratings.

The Mark 15 weighed only 57 pounds. Comparatively a Johnson 10 weighed 60 lbs, a Scott-Atwater 10 weighed 59 lbs and a Martin 10 weighed 58 lbs. Evinrude did not build a 10 HP outboard in 1953 but according to the 1985 catalog a new 9.9 HP standard length, rope starting model weighs 72 lbs.

The Mark 15 and 20 are viewed by many ardent outboarders today as being classics in design and style. Indeed modern motors must search long and hard to surpass these thirty-plus-year-old outboards in any category. Perhaps quietness and powerhead accessibility are the only two areas hwere they may have the edge.

The Mark 20 would evolve through the 1950's, but curiously the Mark 15 began and ended its life in 1953, leaving this Mercury class "A" sized engine as having the shortest production run of any Merc up until that time. The Mark 20 outboard outsold the 15 many times over as most people evidently choose more power in the same trim package. Though the "A" motor was out of production, race drivers were not faced with a shortage of engines. Racers simply began to acquire stock KG-4's and Mark 15's and add the quicksilver lower units and tower housings which Mercury Still produced. Incidently this class "A" powerhead is still very much alive and winning races, although at this late date parts are admittedly hard to locate.

If you happen to see a Mark 15 tucked away somewhere give this old outboard a second glance. We are not likely to see its kind come our way again.

ANTIQUE CORNER

by

Lawrence Carpenter

1934 Johnson Model A-70

In 1934 Johnson Motors was in very serious difficulty. Of course the same could have been said for many companies during this period, but the troubles at Johnson were partially of their own making.

The fall of 1929 found the company heavily committed to the future. Investment in the form of promotion and new model tooling was high. There was every reason for this as business had been very good. Indeed had it not been for the recent formation of OMC, Johnson Motors would have remained the largest producer of outboards in the world.

It was after the stock market crash that serious errors in judgement were made by Johnson management. The company chose to disregard this forewarning of economic distress and assume a business as usual stance, believing that better times were just around the corner. This school of thought was not peculiar to Johnson alone, but was held by many firms. The results were almost always disasterous.

Plans for 1930 were carried forth which included the marketing of matched boat and motor units, fully outfitted for immediate use. It is questionable whether such a concept would have been successful even in good times as people seemed to prefer to create their own boat and motor combinations. For those who had the money a buyers market held endless possibilities. Furthermore, the mechanics of the matched unit program were fraught with competitive disadvantages and its failure was undeniable.

The next few years saw Johnson slip closer toward total collapse, however the company continued to field a complete line of quality outboards.

For 1934 a detailed and comprehensive, red, white, and blue folder announced the new motors which ranged from a 1.4HP single to the powerful 26.1HP, 4-cylinder model "V" series engine. A total of seven horsepower choices presented in three groups were offered. Group II was comprised of the model A-70 pictured here and the larger 9.2HP model K-70. Both these outboards were alternate firing twins, a design Johnson had pioneered in 1930 as part of their "forward at any cost" thinking. Unlike the company's boat-motor combinations, these new outboards were a marked success although the revenue they produced could not stem the firms downhill slide.

The cost of the 4.1HP Johnson Sea Horse model A-70 in 1934 was $140.00. The price of this motor, like the rest, had fluctuated drastically over the previous five years. In 1930 the model A alternate twin had debuted at $160.00 only to drop to $145.00 by 1932. In 1933 the figure fell to $124.50, but apparently in 1934 the company felt the market might bear an increase. After all, this exclusive design had proved itself and was available only from Johnosn.

The advertizing folder elaborated as follows: "The World-famed Alternate Firing Twin --- pioneered by Johnson and possessing a finished perfection that comes only with years of experience in building this type of motor. A deluxe outboard -- providing the upmost in smooth powerflow and brilliant performance".

The list of standard features of the A-70 convinced many outboarders that this motor was for them. A special protection clutch afforded an added safeguard against propeller damage. Spark and throttle controls were synchronized with one lever. Vacuum pressure cooling (no water pump) was provided along with watercooled underwater exhaust. A rubber mounted steering handle controlled the new patented co-pilot which automatically held the A-70 on a given course. With the instant pivot reverse the motor could be rotated 360 degrees. A new propeller shaft seal along with the proven rotary valve breathing system completed the picture.

The "A" model continued on for a few more years until in the late thirties it was replaced with a new series. However, by that time other, more basic changes had been effected. In the fall of 1935 Outboard Motors Corporation purchased a controlling interest in the Johnson Motor Company and the following year Johnson became a division of a newly created entity, Outboard Marine and Manufacturing Corporation.

Evinrude-Elto and Johnson continued to market totally separate lines of outboards until 1951 when both divisons unveiled their new 25HP models. These motors were identical except for minor details such as shroud style, color, and name. The following year the divisions repeated the process with the tiny 3HP twin.

Through most of the 1950's Evinrude and Johnson shared production of the four intermediate models. Evinrude marketed the 7½ and 15HP motors. Johnson dealers sold a 5½ and a 10. Near the end of the decade, however, the models of both divisions complemented each other from top to bottom.

The parent company, now simply Outboard Marine Corporation, has continued this tradition to the present day. Evinrude and Johnson outboards remain at the forefront of an American industry that now faces competition from several foreign makers. However, Americans have never shied away from healthy competition and the Americah built outboard motor shall remain the world standard by which others are measured. Heck, even during the less-than-favorable conditions of 1934 the Johnson A-70 was one of the very best outboard motors in its class.

ANTIQUE CORNER

by

LAWRENCE CARPENTER

Gar Wood

Though none of these sleek mahogany boats have been produced since the late 1940's, the name recognition of Gar Wood is startling. Indeed this fame has spread beyond any boating fraternity then or now as a high percentage of people young and old have heard something of this man and his deeds or the extensive line of pleasure craft he built. There are many fine examples of Gar Wood hulls still to be found and happily more are being resurrected and restored every year, so let us take a brief look at the man himself.

Born in 1881 in Iowa, Garfield Arthur Wood received an education which finally centered on the engineering sciences. This background coupled with a creative and inventive mind was to produce a considerable fortune while he was still quite young.

While living in Detroit, he invented a hydralic hoist to be used on those very early dump trucks. Revenue from this invention and others in the field of road building equipment and even oil fired furnaces allowed Gar, as he was nicknamed, the opportunity to persue a hobby which would make him world famous in a few short years. Garfield Wood found himself completely taken with those early powerboats, but more particularly he was interested in speed.

His early efforts were in the 10 to 15 MPH range, however in 1910 he set his first world's record. Gar Wood's actual racing career really got under way when in 1917, driving his Miss Detroit II, he set a new American speed record of over 61 MPH and won the Gold Cup in the process. From then on Gar Wood sought an even greater challenge; namely the British International Harmsworth Trophy.

The Harmsworth Trophy represented world supremacy in motorboat racing. The trophy was originally donated to Britains Royal Motor Yacht Club by Irish born newspaper publisher Sir Alfred Harmsworth in 1903. The deed of gift stipulated that the trophy, a bronze plaque depicting two turn-of-the-century powerboats rounding a buoy in rough water, be competed for by boat teams representing countries rather than individuals. The trophy was always open to challenge by boats under forty feet in length and with the exception of that period during World War I such a challenge was issued on a fairly regular basis until 1934. Trophy rules stated that competing craft be constructed from components originating from the represented country, so in the case of powerplants this rule narrowed the field of contenders to those possessing high powered aircraft engines which were almost always used in these boats.

The last displacement hull to win the Harmsworth did so in 1910. In 1911 the stepped hydroplane type hull came to dominate all subsequent races. These boats were not of the same configuration familiar today, but rather sleek speedboat types with one or more steps built into the planing surface.

In 1920 competition was resumed. And Gar Wood was ready. His newly built Miss America was among the three United States challengers to journey to England as the British craft Maple Leaf IV had won the last trophy race in 1913 as it had the two previous years.

With Gar Wood driving and his mechanic, Orlin Johnson seated beside him, Miss America brought the Harmsworth Trophy back to the U.S. after a ten year absence. Over the next thirteen year period Gar Wood successfully defended the Trophy seven times with a total of ten Miss

America boats. The last of these, Miss America $\overline{X}$, was powered by four 1600 HP Packard engines and established a world speed record of 102.256 MPH in 1930. On Sept. 20, 1932 Gar Wood and this same Miss America $\overline{X}$ increased the mark to 124.915 MPH on the St. Clair River near Algonac Michigan. Gar Wood's Miss Americas were not always the fastest boats in the race, however they were the most durable. One recurrent problem of the English craft particularly was their insistence on channeling multi engine power into one gearbox.

Gar Wood's last defense of the Harmsworth was in 1933 whereupon he retired from racing. Curiously, The English retired also as had the French earlier in the 1920's. Indeed there would not be another challenge for the Trophy for 16 years.

Gar Wood's activities during these years included much more than the defense of the Harmsworth Trophy. Wood's early boats were built by Chris Smith (Chris Craft) & Sons Boat Co at Algonac. Later, Gar Wood purchased the plant and began manufacturing the boats himself. Under pressure from friends and other boating sportsmen Gar began turning out high speed creations for those whose taste in boats was the same as his own. Soon luxury runabouts capable of performing gracefully and safely in the 55 MPH speed range were being offered.

Gar Woods expertise and business sense was always garnished with a flare for the dramatic. In 1921, piloting his cruiser Gar Jr. II, he beat a fast express train in a race from New York to Miami by four minutes. Later in 1924 he bettered the Twentieth Century Limited from New York to Albany by nine minutes.

By the late twenties, after several plant expansions, the facilities at Algonac still proved inadequate. Thus, in January of 1930 the new Gar Wood plant, the first modern, fireproof facility built solely for the manufacture of stock runabouts was occupied at Marysville, Michigan.

L. Carpenter

Its production capability was 1200 boats a year.

Gar Wood boats were among the very finest built anywhere and this was at a time when quality was the rule rather than the exception. During the late twenties Gar Woods were of the large and super speed variety, their length in the 26 to 33 foot range with some speeds touching 60 MPH. As time went on smaller runabouts were offered until in 1934 the 16' models was introduced. This diminutive craft was constructed of the same high grade meterials and with the same attention to detail as were the larger boats.

Top-of-the-line model of the Gar Wood fleet was the 40 foot cruiser.

The company survived the Depression better than most. A firm capital base and sound management was instrumental in allowing Gar Woods to be built and sold in sufficient numbers to carry the company through these lean years. By the mid to late 1930's production was back up to that banner year in 1929 with model selection far surpassing that which was available at that time. By the early 1940's prospective customers could choose from well over 100 Gar Wood models.

Admittedly, the preceeding has hardly made a dent in all that can and should be said about Gar Wood. In the future we will take a closer look at specific boats of the Gar Wood line.

While still a teenager in the late fifties I was the proud owner of a mid-thirties vintage Gar Wood 28-foot custom runabout for most of a fall boating season. The boat had been for sale for some time at the marina at which I worked. The asking price was somewhere around $800. The boat, though not in mint condition, was still in very good shape. The upholstory had been professionally done quite recently although naugahyde was used intead of the original leather. The boat looked good and ran well. I had driven it a few time and fallen in love with it. After buying the Gar Wood for considerably less than the asking price I became acutely aware of how much gas the 200 HP Scripps engine required to push the old boat down the lake at a respectable speed. Consequently, I did not use the boat as much as I wanted to. Further I was facing winter storage costs as I knew I could not handle the boat at home. Selling that big old Gar Wood is not one of my fondest memories.

DESIGNER'S CONCEPT

by

Lawrence C. Carpenter

The SUSPENDED HYDRA-TRACK

We've been through a lot. Ever since we got on plane we've tried nearly everything. Flat bottom, step-plane, shallow vee, three pointers, deep vee, cathredral, tunnel, and more. We have cast every conceivable shape upon the waters -- or have we?

In the wake of this query comes the Suspended Hydra-Track and the promotional material continues along these lines.

The speed of a three point hydro; the ride of a tunnel hull; the stability of a deep vee and it tracks like its on rails. All this would be more than enough, but the real thrill comes when you turn the wheel.

The Hydra-Track is like no other high performance hull to come down the river. First of all, the boat is steered from the front with its outboard locked in a straight-on position. The torsion bar suspended sponsons have a twenty degree deflection capability and specially designed running surfaces that permit the Hydra-Track to turn as no other boat ever has. The variable suspension further allows the driver to tune the hull to water conditions at a moments notice, to afford much improved comfort over choppy seas.

For tight turns at off-plane speeds or super sharp turns at speeds above, the outboard is released when the sponsons reach their 20 degree port or starboard lock to perform its normal turning function. However, the motor remains straight while the sponsons are within their 40 degree arc. The steering sponsons will actually deliver considerable bow deflection when the boat is at an absolute standstill.

Try driving your car in reverse down the road for a mile or two and then contemplate that this is how you've been steering your boat all along. The Hydra-Track experience is like nothing else afloat.

Characteristics of the hull proper are those of a modified tunnel concept with extra lift capability astern. Bottom configuration at the transom bites and holds in the sharper turns, yet is free and fast on the straights.

The Hydra-Track is designed for safety as well as performance. High speed night boating accidents are on the rise and the results are often tragic. The H-T can see and be seen with a new lighting system built into the hull. The oversize red and green running lights located within the leading edges of the boat are extra bright and can be seen for miles. Further in toward the bow are mounted two powerful headlights, their angle of attack adjustable from the drivers seat to compensate for hull trim. These lights are not intended to take the place of the traditional spotlight, but can be used on a more full time basis. Many more boaters are finding themselves in unfamiliar waters these days and in a variety of instances these lights are a must.

The Suspended Hydra-Track is not going to sweep other sport runaboutstypes from the boating scene. It will certainly not hold its own with a deep-vee in heavy seas. And it may not keep up with a record seeking hydroplane streaking through a straight course under ideal conditions. However, we are a breed who deal in specialities and we welcome specific machines that will do particular tasks well. One would not, after all, drive their Ferrari up that poor excuse of a logging road that one just came down with their four-wheel-drive Jeep. The Hydra-Track is a new concept of sport hull designed to perform as no other has within a range of boating that is really not all that narrow. Possibly in the near future we can find out just how well it does.

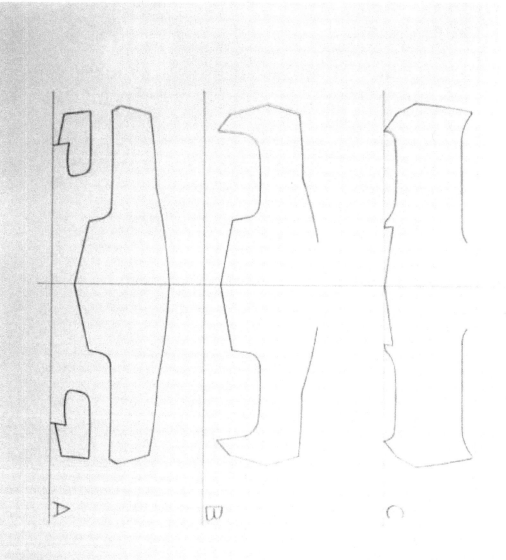

ANTIQUE CORNER
by
LAWRENCE CARPENTER

1948 Evinrude Lightfour

The Lightfour is the fourth in the series of five Evinrude four-cylinder outboards discussed in this column over the past three years. The Sportfour, March 1982; The Big Four, November 1982; and the Zephur, January 1984.

In 1948, this engine, like the Zephur and Big Four was near the end of its production run. The opposed firing fours and twins of Outboard Motors Corporation had planted their roots over a decade before. Though still good, solid and servicable motors, these designs had become outdated at this point in time as other, more compact and efficient outboards began to appear after the war. Indeed, the war had injected a four or five year delay into the evolution of the outboard motor, however some companies were affected more than others.

Mercury had recently arrived on the scene when the war really got underway and not being tied to an extensive model line, found its war-time activities centering around pure engine development which would prove extremely useful later on. Conversely, OMC produced a complete and varied selection of outboards. The military quickly found that it required these motors in large numbers and though civilian outboard production was stopped by federal order early in 1942, the manufacture of many models continued. There wasn't time to modernize or add features that might have lured prospective buyers. The Armed Forces needed engines immidiately and the existing designs hastely modified for military use would prove more than adequate.

For this reason OMC was still marketing some of these older designs during the late 1940's until newer motors could take their place. And boaters didn't seem to mind. Recreational products of all kinds were in high demand and outboards like the Lightfour sold very well.

This edition of the Lightfour was essentially the same motor that made its debut back in 1934 as one of the two Evinrudes that ushered in the new wave of "Hooded Power". At that time, it was known as the "Imperial" Lightfour, however over the years this outboard dropped its regal title and assumed a role of versatility. The Lightfour was very smooth running and would sustain a slow troll for hours. Rated at nearly 10 HP it would also plane small skiffs and runabouts, making it popular with fisherman who wanted to get there in a hurry or with those in the mood for some summer fun afloat.

The Lightfour was also prepared to handle more serious chores. This outboard could be ordered with either a five-inch or fifteen-inch extended shaft making it applicable to larger hull types for work or play. A further option was a heavy-duty lower unit providing a slower gear ratio and swinging a larger prop able to push heavy loads. The Lightfour was a favorite workboat motor for these reasons. Also, it was a popular choice to power outboard cruisers of the non-planing type where a leisurely speed of 10 - 12 mph was considered sufficient.

In 1948 Evinrude was pushing its new Sportsman and Sportwin motors at the bottom of its six engine line-up. The Lightfour remained much the same as it had in 1934. A more streamlined gas tank, shroud, and muffler assembly had modernized its appearance somewhat, but mechanically there had been few changes.

However, enough of downplaying this outboard and let's mention a few of its fine qualities, some of which compare favorably with todays outboards. The Lightfour developed 9.7 HP from 15 cubic inches, not a bad ratio when looking at motors produced a decade or more later. This outboard was one of the last to utilize cast iron cylinder blocks, however its weight was listed at a mere 66 pounds. Though for some reason the Lightfour pictured here weighs closer to 70 lbs, this is still less than new models in the same power range. Incidently, if one checks the weights of new outboards with those produced as much as fifty years ago one will find that horsepower for horsepower the new ones are often heavier, some drastically so. Curious to say the least!

The lower unit of the Lightfour is as smooth and efficient as those found on most present day motors. But then OMC has always been a leader in this category of outboard design. The Lightfour featured a twist grip throttle control when other, more modern, motors of the day did not. But here again, Evinrude pioneered the twist grip throttle in the late twenties. The Lightfour did not have a full gear shift. But then neither did other outboards. Johnson and Scott Atwater would introduce this feature a year later.

This particular Lightfour is in excellent original condition, having been run perhaps ten or fifteen hours. It had been advertised as part of an estate sale in a neighboring state. A friend and fellow Antique Outboard Motor Club member saw the ad, but unavoidably arrived late in the day after nearly all the merchandise had been sold. He was surprised to find this engine still on the premises, sequestered in a closet where it had been for may years. The owner was very glad to sell the engine for a very reasonable price and the antique outboarder, being impressed with the engines condition, bought the outboard. However, after a few months he reconsidered and sold the engine to me remarking that the Lightfour didn't really fit into his collection.

Indeed the sight of a Lightfour will produce only a yawn from most antique outboarders. Though not quite as common as its smaller cousin, the Zephyr, the Lightfour is only slightly more popular. I must confess that I have gone along with the crowd, for in the past I have sold, traded, or given away Lightfours at the least provocation.

This old outboard really deserves much better treatment. Although more complex than other engines of its size, the Lightfour is a strong and reliable performer in a rugged forties style that could become popular again if given the chance. Certainly nothing like it is being produced today, nor will ever be again. I have to admit, I like this outboard more every time I look at it.

SPECIFICATIONS

Engine Type	opposed four cylinders
Bore & Stroke	1-3/4" X 1-35/64"
Cubic Inches	15
Horsepower	9.7 @ 4000 RPM
Fuel Capacity	1½ gallons
Top Speed - Light Runabouts	25 MPH
Propeller Protection	Rubber cusioned drive
Carburetor	Float Feed Auto-type with Silencer, Indicator Dial and Flash Start Primer
Weight	66 pounds
Cost	$260.00

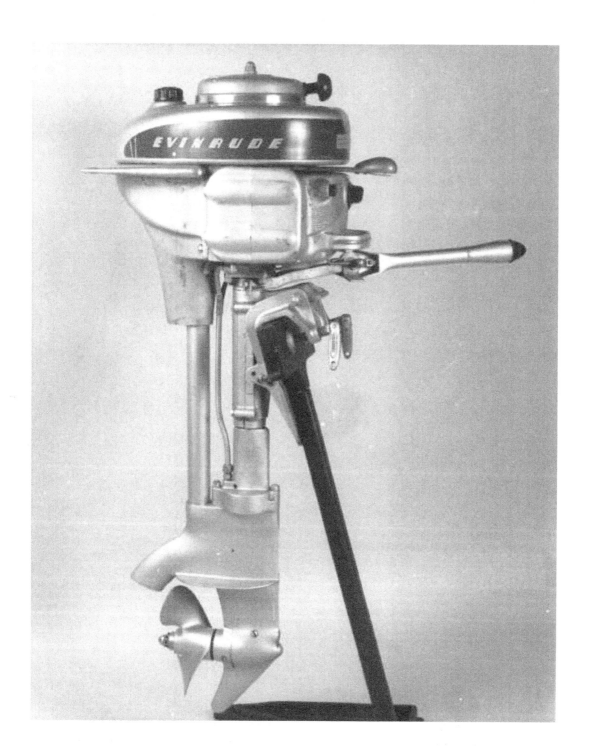

ANTIQUE CORNER

by

LAWRENCE CARPENTER

1933 OMC 4-60

(A Future Restoration, Part I)

This old racing engine represents a departure from those outboards usually appearing in this column. This motor is something of a mess. At this time it remains in the same condition as it was when it came in the door a few months ago and thus presents an opportunity to touch upon a few points that must be considered when restoring an outboard such as this.

Last fall the motor was found residing peacefully at a Johnson dealership along the coast of Maine where it had been for some time. As it happened, the owner had collected several old Johnsons and was happy to trade this beast for an uncommon model of that make built during the mid-twenties. Unfortunately any story or history relating to the 4-60 had been forgotten long ago.

The number of this top-of-the-line racing engine is 8280124. The first three digits are the model number from which the type of motor and year of manufacture are deduced. The 0124 is the number of this engine indicating that it was the 124th 4-60 produced in 1933. One might think that this is a low number, however in conversing with a few 4-60 experts around the country one discovers that this number is very high. This was a very limited production, and to a high degree, hand-built machine. They didn't make all that many. Incidently, 4-60 translates to 4 cylinders, 60 cubic inches.

Actually this outboard is in quite good condition overall considering that is is a racing engine and therefore would ha-e been a prime candidate for creative rigging and modification as one searched for a little more speed. This particular motor has escaped certain changes that one might expect, yet has a couple others that appear strange and probably relate certain information about the engines past use.

First of all, this motor was factory equipped with a Linkert carburetor in 1932 and 33 - or was it 33 and 34? Anyway, the Linkert was nearly always taken off in favor of a Vacturi-500 unit which worked somewhat better. Yet the carb on this 4-60 is another Vacturi model usually found on some Johnson 50 cubic inch 4 cylinder, "V" series service motors. It is unlikely that this old girl would have been raced successfully with this carburetor.

It is strange that this motor still retains its factory exhaust system which includes standard type exhaust manifolds and a somewhat relieved muffler can. Early photos prove that the 4-60 was raced with this paraphanalia, but its likely that it would have been discarded after a short while in favor of more free flowing exhaust headers or simple deflectors.

The 4-60 was not equipped with a tiller handle, but rather a rear mounted steering bar for use with a steering wheel and control cables. The bar this engine came with was an ugly, homemade excuse for a decent such component and it si the one item I have taken off and thrown away.

Another oddity, but yet a pleasant surprise as with the original exhaust system, is that the lower unit is the one that came with the motor and it has survived untampered with or modified. Such happenings were common as a racing motor evolved with age.

Any conclusions? There is often-heard statement that goes something like ---"if only such and such an inanimate object could talk". Well in this case the old 4-60 may have said something. It seems likely that the motor may have seen a short racing career and then used as a service hot rod, raceabout, have-fun-with motor utilized in more non-sanctioned mayhem or maybe just putting around.

Might this be good or bad from the view-point of someone planning to restore the outboard to as-new condition? It may not be worn out but it may have been misused. Things can get very interesting if you're an old outboard nut. And if you're not, you can learn.

Let us proceed. The sparkplugs in the engine now are a much higher heat range than the specified Champion K5812 or K57R, but this clue is inconclusive as the plugs could easily have been switched at any time. Looking further we find that when turning the engine over by hand the bearings feel very good with little apparent wear.

The engine has excellent compression especially since its dry as a bone. But what's this? The bottom pair of cylinders on this opposed firing four appear to have considerably less compression that the upper pair. Though the 1933 model was the first to be equipped with a formal water pump, this engine was not designed to cool properly at less than planing speeds maintained for more than a minute or so. As a sport-service outboard it is more likely that the motor might have seen such use and therefore gotten a little too hot for its own good. The lower cylinders would get hot first and the required tension may have been cooked from these piston rings. Some may have become stuck in their grooves. Not good, but possibly not all that serious.

It is not clear if the 1933 4-60 came factory equipped with an external oil tank and drip feed system which metered additional oil into the crankcase although it is apparent that this system was used on most of these motors. Specified gas-oil mix ran as high as one quart of oil per gallon with more fed from the tank, This was a lot of oil. Another, even rarer, 4-60 model sported double ignition to combat plug fouling, however the model 828 would handle such a mixture when properly tuned as would other high performance motors of the day.

This motor does not have the external oil system although some in-place amateur piping indicates that it did have at one time. Possibly it was removed when the motor became just a fun outboard and further, maybe the oil mix was reduced even more to cut expenses. The 4-60 would tolerate less oil, but not if it was pushed hard.

One last complication regarding the correctness of an oil tank is the fact that later in the 1930's O.M.C. built the 4-60 with roller bearings on the center main thus eliminating the need for so much oil. These bearings were accepted by the earlier engines and many still in service were updated with the later bearings.

One might ask why not look at a catalog picture of the engine? Well, the catalog shot for the 4-60 is the rear-quarter view of the starboard side. The oil tank, if its there, is hidden from sight. Furthermore, these pictures are nearly always retouched, may be out-of-date, and are frequently inaccurate in some way. Other advertising shots of racing motors in the water cannot be considered because once these engines were clamped on the back of a racing hull all bets were off concerning originality.

The lack of good photographic record rears its ugly head in other areas as well. The absence of any trace of a gas tank decal on this engine is a good example. Indeed the only original finish to be found here is on the underside of the tank where the factory bright orange paint remains intact. The decal surrounded the entire four gallon tank, It was about three feet long and somewhat over four inches wide and it represents a major part of the cosmetic restoration of this motor. None of these decals exist or are being reproduced, so it must be made from scratch. Decal style was changed every year. The tank sides always displayed the numbers 4-60 in one form or another, however evidence suggests that the Elto name as well as the OMC insignia may have appeared on the rear tank face depending on how the engine was marketed.

Next month we will consider some specific steps to be taken in the restoration of this old racing outboard and here I would like to welcome comments from any readers having specific knowledge of this old racing machine.

Unlike other hobbies that have been thoroughly researched over a long period of time by countless idividuals, antique outboards have received considerably less attention.
This is one reason that these old kickers are so enjoyable. New facts and information are constantly surfacing. No one knows it all and those of us involved with these old motors are geateful for additional peices of the puzzle.

I'm sure there are still a great many old 4-60 drivers out there. Just how many can go all the way back to this particular model remains to be seen. However, any help received in putting this old outboard back the way it was when left it the factory will be apprecaited by us all.

ANTIQUE CORNER

by

Lawrence Carpenter

1933 OMC 4-60

(A Future Restoration, Part II)

The restoration of an old racing outboard allows one certain latitudes. Some modifications or the inclusion of other-than-original equipment or accessories may be acceptable if they represent the configuration in which the engine was actually raced. Many of these changes were indeed factory constructed and approved and therefore lend further interest to the motor. However if one intends to duplicate the condition of the motor as it was originally built, standards must be somewhat more rigid.

Predictably, the first step will be to dissamble the outboard, at least to the point where its inner workings may be thoroughly inspected. If as suspected, bearings, lower unit gears, etc are in good shape, a total rebuild of these components may not be necessary, or even advisable.

Several parts on this outboard were nickel plated and these must be shipped out to a reputable plater to be re-nickeled. The flywheel and flywheel nut, the main water tube, cylinder water fittings and muffler shell complete this picture except for the cylinders. These must be plated also, but not totally. Economics were a prime consideration in 1933. Thus, only the ends of the cylinders to a point about an inch around on the sides were nickeled. The remaining area was painted bleck. Detailed instructions must be given the plater regarding this work or one can simply have the entire surface plated and then paint over 80 % of the area - not a pleasant thought when one considers that there is between two and three hundred dollars worth of nickel on this engine. While the plating is being done other parts of the engine may be restored.

All aluminium castings having a cast finish must be cleaned to appear

L.. Carpenter

to be right out of the mold. These include the transom clamp, crank case, driveshaft housing, pump housing, rope plate, coil mounts, etc. The cast aluminum muffler ends are painted black, however one of these must be repaired first. In using a non-stock gas tank fitting someone had seen fit to saw off a good portion of the uppermost cooling fin to allow extra space. Therefore, the missing piece must be reproduced, welded into place, and its finish made consistent with that of the remainder of the part..

Polished aluminum parts must be highly buffed to a bright shine. Of these parts, the lower unit is the largest and most basic and here we have an added problem. It is evident that the 4-60 had lain on its backside in a damp area, possibly in the dirt outside, for a long period of time at some point in its long history. The rear of the cavitation plate and its support are badly corroded and must be heavily sanded, then polished. Other support points during the engines long rest were the muffler extension studs, which must be reproduced and the formed aluminum gas tank which has corroded completely through in the rear starboard corner.

Mechanically the lower unit feels to be in good adjustment and condition, however, the case will be split to visually inspect gears, ets. If wear appears to be within acceptable limits the unit will be closed and packed with lubricant.

The $10\frac{1}{2}$" x $17\frac{1}{2}$" two blade bronze prop is somewhat dinged up, but not really out of shape. If this was a service motor or an older, slower turning outboard I would repair the prop myslef, but in view of the 6000 RPM this engine turns, the propeller will be sent out to be professionally reconditioned.

The mechanics of the powerhead will be closely inspected with special focus on bearings, piston rings and cylinder bores. Not much can be said here without knowing what we're getting into, but I will venture a couple of opinions based on what I think I'll find.

I don't intend to rebuild the powerhead as a matter of course, but only if necessary. If the bearings are as good as they feel I don't plan to dissassemble everything. These engines were basically hand built and I would rather leave things as they are than disrupt the position of say, some of the individual rollers. The rings are something else again. If they are not badly worn they will at least have lost much of their spring tension. In this case they will be removed from the piston and lightly peened to regain the tension they have lost. This process is not used much these days and warrants a brief explanation. The ring is placed upright on a hard flat surface and is lightly struck at many evenly spaced locations around its inside diameter with a proper tool. This action stretches the metal and forces the ring open again. There is more to the process, but generally that's it. One must be very careful as it is easy to break a ring. Light honing is sometimes necessary to remove any thickness distortion done in peening and the ring is placed back on the piston in the same position and location that it was in originally. Compression in engines where wear is not really extensive is often much better after peening the rings than installing new ones, honing the cylinders, and going through a sometimes tricky break-in period although such may not be the case with newer motors of modern design.

The 4-60's ignition system will require some serious attention. First of all, it must be completely rewired using a correct reproduction of the original wire types. There is presently no spark on the bottom two cylinders. Although the trouble may well be the points located in the timer under the flywheel, it is likely that the condensors and possibly both coils will have to be replaced if they don't prove to be up to par. This will not be a pleasant job as these last items are located in the cylindrical case located under the carburetor. The coils and condensors are packed in a non-conductive, tar-like goo within the cylinder.

The gas tank and particularly the three-foot-long decal will be one of the more difficult parts of the restoration. Fortunately the tank is not badly dented. Usually tanks on larger heavier outboards are found in better condition than those on smaller motors. The reason for this is simply that the lighter fishing type engines were taken off the boat and moved about a great deal making the fragile tanks more susceptable to damage. However, we'll still have to get inside the tank to repair a few dents and remove some corrosion. This means sawing out a section of the tank large enough to allow free movement of one hand inside. The location of this area to be removed can be the bottom of the tank or sometimes the middle forward section behind the flywheel. In the case of the 4-60 this latter site is not all that well hidden from view thus exposing the finish weld, so the bottom section between the tank mounts is the spot to choose. Though a complication here is the fact that the aluminum muffler heat shield is tack welded to the mounts in six places and must be sawed free before the tank can be gotten into..But then the reinstallation of the shield will hide the tank weld.

When a smooth finish on the exterior of the tank is regained the removed door is welded shut once more. The tank is then primed and painted its original bright orange color.

The correct reproduction of the decal could well be a story in itself, but for now I can only say that more research will have to be done to discover exactly what it looked like.

Compromises. Ah, yes. There are likely to be some along the way. The original Linkert carb may not be found, so the Vacturi 500 model will have to be used. It is, after all, correct in its usage. The external oil system? We will find out if its necessary when I look at that center main crankshaft bearing.

Well there are a few of the expected highlights. The purpose in my mind is not to remanufacture the entire engine, but to restore around those areas that remain in acceptable condition thus preserving more of this old outboards original historical value. The engine will be run to its fullest, but not raced hard.

As mentioned previously, no one knows it all, so any suggestions or help from anyone who holds a piece of the puzzle is most welcome.

Next year this old 4-60 will make one last appearance in this column. It should look quite different than it does now.

ANTIQUE CORNER

by

Lawrence Carpenter

THE CHRIS CRAFT COBRA

As the 1950's got under way stylists contemplated the shape of things to come. Americans had money to spend and manufacturers were quick to realize that a modernistic design would catch the eye of prospective customers. After World War II people had wanted a fresh start and the Korean conflict did little to quell this attitude. The immediate post war designs were already wearing thin and clearly a no-holds-barred, skies-the-limit approach would dictate success at the market place. Old was out and new was in as Americans sought to make up for lost time and surround themselves with futuristic shapes.

Perhaps nowhere were the results more dramatic than in the auto industry. Indeed some cars produced during the latter part of the decade looked like they had been let out of a cage. However, even in their extreme, many designs were very well done and are much sought after today as they reflect an uninhibited freedom of style that we are unlikely to see again. Some of these super-large sports models were actually referred to as "boats". Other cars of the period were a garish mess then as now. A "58" Olds anyone?

These adventures in styling were certainly not lost on the boating industry. Even during the War years many companies offered full page renderings in leading boating magazines to illustrate their far-out intentions once hostilities had ceased. To be sure, few of these concepts were ever manufactured, but the impression of an entire industry straining at the leash of an imposed wartime footing was established in the minds of an eager boat buying public.

During the early to mid 1950's when stylists hurridly shifted gears from the rounded, somewhat bulbous school of design to the developing sleek and low forward looking, finned projectile concepts, the boating industry was ready and more than willing. Once again some models seemed to offer shock value alone as if to test the public eye to see how much it could take. For the most part such craft were built by smaller companies hoping to make a big splash in an expanding market, but the older, more established firms were not slow to react either. Generally, these latter concerns tried to blend their classic traditions with the wave of the future and many of these boats were pure excitement to behold.

Perhaps no one accomplished this task to a finer degree than the men at Chris Craft. In 1954 the Chris Chraft Cobra model was conceived and by fall of that year pictures of this sleek, single seat runabout were seen in many boating publications. Production of the 18 and 21 foot editions of the Cobra commenced in mid January, 1955.

The Cobra was not merely a jazzed up version of an existing model, but an entirely new boat. The first Chris Craft model to employ the use of fiberglass, the Cobras golden tail fin and engine hatches were molded from this material. The stylish dark mahogany hull was accented with the familiar blond Chris Craft trim and also present was a more rakish version of the traditional bull nose atop the forward tilting stem. Both Cobras were single seat sport boats. The eighteen footer could accomodate three people. The twenty-one, with an added eight inches of beam, could squeeze in a fourth.

The most popular of the two engines options available with the eighteen was the 131 HP Chris Craft powerplant. Top speed so equipped was about 40 mph. The twentyone could be had with one of three engines, the largest being a 285 HP Cadillac V-8. Speed here was in the 55 mph range.

A complete array of equipment came standard on the Cobra. Complete instrumentation, of course, as well as an automatic bilge pump, fire extinguisher, tool kit and more. Options included air horns, siren, cockpit cover, full covers, and spotlight among others. Prospective buyers could order the Cobra custom built to include their own personal touch or special engine installation and several boats left the factory so modified.

Strange and unfortunate is the fact that the Cobra production was very short lived. The last of these classic sport hulls left the Chris Craft plant in mid September of 1955 with scarcely more than 50 boats of each model being built. Strange, but then General Motors gave serious thought to dropping the Corvette after a poor initial showing about the same period.

The Cobra was but a single sport boat suited for high speed cruising and little else. Water skiing was akward to say the least as were other boat associated activities that the 1955 buyer indulged in. That and a high price tag ($6500.00 plus for the Cad powered twenty-one) are thought to be reasons for the early demise of the Cobra. But then also, the Cobra may have been a bit too early. Had possibly the boat been offered a couple of years later in 1957? Well, who knows?

Howard and Dolores Tubbs of Hyde Park, NY are the proud owners of the eighteen-foot Cobra Sneaky Snake, pictured here. She is hull number 50 and therefore one of the last produced. Purchased by the Tubbs in the spring of 1981 this Cobra was in a sad state of disarray being partially disassembled and her original engine gone. The boat has since been restored to factory specifications and has taken many awards at antique and classic boat shows.

Robert C. Davis, 1121 Clinton, Algonac, Michigan and his wife Mary are also among the many present day Cobra fans who, like the Tubbs of Hyde Park, own one of the all-too-few eighteen foot editions. Robert is attempting to compile a current list of all existing Cobras. An accurate account of surviving boats from a total production of 108 including the prototypes is still forthcoming. So if you find you own one of these sweethearts, no matter what her condition, please contact him if you haven't already. Even if you think yours or the one you know of is beyond hope rest assured that there are those out there in classic boat land who are prepared to spare nothing in order to resurrect even one more Chris Craft Cobra.

For those who find they have an interest in old Chris Craft's in general or even one specific model in particular, the Chris Craft Antique Boat Club might be for you. Their address is 217 South Adams St., Tallahassee, Florida. They would like to hear from you and chances are you'll like what they have to say.

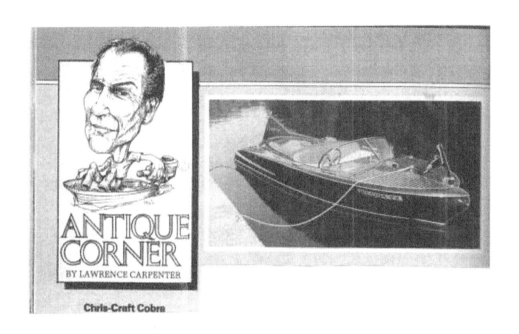

ANTIQUE CORNER
BY LAWRENCE CARPENTER

Chris-Craft Cobra

ANTIQUE CORNER

by

LAWRENCE CARPENTER

The Johnson Tilting Stern Drive
and Early I.O.'s in General

For most of us, the mention of the now familiar inboard-outboard marine propulsion configuration is likely to drag our memory back to the late 1950's when these units were gaining in popularity. Reaching back in time from this point one recalls the predominence of the straight-shafted inboards with an ocassional vee drive tossed in for variety.

Well, once again there proves to be little that is truly new under the sun, or in this case on the water and we find that the I.O. design is several decades older than it is commonly thought to be today. Indeed the concept itself can be traced back to the turn of the century, but by 1930 companies such as Columbian, Ludington, and Johnson had produced inboard-outboard units very similar in appearance to those currently in use.

However, almost as soon as they began to appear several factors combined to nearly eliminate the I.O. or stern drive from the marketplace. Some reasons for this were an economic sign of the times. Other explanations centered around the technical limitations of the units themselves.

Advantages of these early I.O. units were of course the same as they are today with superior maneuverability topping the list. But these units were much heavier than their modern counterparts as upper housings and gearcases were frequently cast from iron or bronze. Furthermore, the units were generally suitable for use with engines of 100 HP or less as they would not stand the strain of the tremendous torque produced by the larger slow turning, long stroke marine powerplants of the day. Consequently the

I.O. was relegated to boats in the twenty-foot range and smaller. Many of these designs could ill afford all that extra weight hanging off the transom with an engine already placed further astern than usual to take advantage of the stern drive concept in the first place. In addition power required by the unit itself was more noticable when subtracted from a small to medium sized powerplant, therefore a similar boat with the same engine equipped with a standard straight driveshaft and rudder was usually faster than one utilizing the stern drive.

The stern drive units were also more expensive than the conventional drive system and again the added cost was harder to absorb in the smaller lower-priced boats in which it was marketed. Moreover, if there was ever a time when this fact alone would prove to be a real detriment in selling a boat it was that period during the Great Depression when most companies were struggling to stay in business.

The Johnson Motor Company, then a major producer of outboard motors, was involved in a major expansion of its activities in the marine field when economic hardship hit the nation and the company's newly introduced tilting stern drive unit debuted during the worst of times. As has been mentioned before, Johnson chose to largely disregard the gloomy business forecast and therefore pushed blindly ahead believing that the market would rebound quickly.

Although the Johnson Tilting Stern Drive could be purchased and installed in an existing boat, the major portion of these units were sold to boat manufacturers to incorporate into one or more hulls in their model line. Several companies that produced small to medium sized inboard runabouts did exactly this and of these perhaps the name most easily recognized today would be Century (Antique Corner September 1984).

Johnson introduced its stern drive to the industry with much fanfare as was common in those days and referred to it as the most important

L. Carpenter

development in the history of motor boating. At a time when no-holds-barred advertizing was still very much in evidence a statement like this only served to encourage the writer to go even further as the following text illustrates. _____ "There comes to every mechanical contrivance used by mankind that epochal improvement representative of the highest embodiment of human achievement, that obsoletes the past and opens a vista of tomorrows extending as far as human conception can visualize. (wow!) --------Such a revolutionary achievement, a product of human aspiration and skill immeasurable in terms of utility alone, now comes to motor boating. All that can be said about the Johnson Tilting Stern Drive --all the facts of superior performance -- are but the simple truth of an engineering accomplishment which will change all present conceptions of basic motor boat construction and performance.
--------So long as mankind goes down to the sea in boats -- particularly of the medium size, faster motor craft -- so long will the new Johnson Tilting Stern Drive principal provide that reliability, safety, high efficiency, and amazing maneuverability which heretofore has been the characteristic of outboard motor driven boats only."

Well, after so eloquent a dissertation as that I am really at a loss to say very much more except to add that for such a masterful achievement, so carved in stone, the Johnson Stern Drive as well as Johnson Motors as an independent company, lasted only a short time longer.

Johnson's formula for announcing the power limitations of the unit to manufacturers and individuals alike was as follows: The brake horsepower of any motor applied to this drive should not be greater than the recommended revolutions divided by 80. Thus, the HP of an engine turning 2500 RPM should not be more than 31 and the HP of an engine turning 4500 RPM was limited to 56. As the more powerful engines of the day tended to develop their full HP at the lower RPM's, this formula might seem rather strange until one realizes that the limitation was directed more at torque than horsepower.

The stern drive unit was held in place by a shear pin which would break if an obstruction was hit, allowing the unit to tilt. A hand lever was also provided to allow the unit to be raised and latched in its tilted position.

The steering range was 35 degrees in either direction. Two models of the unit were built. One carried a drum for use with steering cables. The other was adapted for rod steering. Gears and shafts were of high grade nickel steel except for the prop shaft which was of stainless steel. Ball bearings were used throughout. The upper gear case and transom plate were cast from malleable iron. The lower gear case of the unit was of a special high tensil strength aluminum alloy.

An anti-torque plate was used to counteract propeller torque. For twin motor installation the drive unit could be turned in either direction and the torque plates adjusted accordingly. Maximum prop diameter was 14 inches. Engine to prop ratio was 1.21 to 1. The tilting section of the unit could be quickly detached from the transom plate by loosening two, rather hefty, wing screws.

Total weight of the stern drive unit was listed at 115 pounds, but several years ago I owned one of these beasts and I could swear that it weighed more than that. I believe my wife Ann would also attest to this as it was she who found it lying in some weeds, procured it from its owner for a few dollars, loaded it into our pickup truck unaided, and brought it home.

The Johnson Stern Drive and other such units of the day may not have been around for long, but they provided a solid base from which others were built in the late 1950's when technology and modern materials allowed for a more efficient unit to be created. Furthermore, the market was ready to accept them in large numbers.

So the next time you see an old fiberglass boat built around 1960 and one of those "early" stern drives, keep in mind that the heritage of these now popular units is somewhat older.

for ALL TOMORROWS

IN MOTOR BOATING

The **JOHNSON TILTING STERN DRIVE**

Written by the same author:

The Public Works
By Lawrence Carpenter

Contact: Ann-Marie Carpenter

P.O. Box 459

Gilmanton, NH 03237

Made in the USA
Las Vegas, NV
04 October 2021